SPEED ADDICTS

GRAND PRIX RACING

a dakini book

MARK HUGHES

SPEED ADDICTS

GRAND PRIX RACING

CollinsWillow

An Imprint of HarperCollins*Publishers*

Published in 2005 by
CollinsWillow
an imprint of HarperCollins*Publishers*
London

First published by dakini books in 2005
© dakini books ltd
www.dakinibooks.com

All images © Sutton Motorsport Images
© Phipps Archive
with thanks to the following whose images are also featured in the book
© Keith Duerden
© Peter Nygard
© Popperfoto Collection

1

A CIP catalogue record for this book
is available from the British Library

ISBN 0 00 721279 8

The HarperCollins website address is
www.harpercollins.co.uk

Printed and bound in Italy

Contents

visco-static
l'huile d'un an
BP
LONGLIFE LON
NQUANT
visco-static
LONGLIF

"Racing is life. Everything else is just waiting"

Early spring 1956. A narrow, bustling Modena terrace. There, a café. Crashing plates, Latin chatter, cigarette smoke mingling with coffee steam. Nestled in the corner, a group of men playing card games, gently taunting each other. One of them – the stocky one with the dangling cigarette, slicked-back hair, false ear and scar, the one who has lived some – is French. He's Jean Behra, serenely filling in time between his duties as a Grand Prix driver for the Maserati team: "I look at my passport, see all the places stamped upon it, look to where it says 'Occupation: Racing Driver' and think, 'Yes, I'm a lucky man'."

Like almost all top racing drivers, his needs were few but psychologically complex. He lived the life millions of men would aspire to 'if only'. If only they'd been born more privileged, if only they didn't have responsibilities. The more honest might say: if only they were braver, more contemptuous of the security promised by society. Behra and his peers, along with the men who raced cars at the highest level 50 years before them, and those who race 50 years after them, did and do so because the urge the sport satisfies is hard-wired into mankind. Those who feel it most do something about it.

Sir Henry Segrave, a Grand Prix winner of the 1920s and twice a holder of the Land Speed Record, claimed: "The attainment of speed is an instinct inherent in the normal human being and in the vast majority of animals, and one which has played a most important part in the process of evolution."

Man was intelligent enough to invent the car and instinctive enough to be racing it soon after. Why should the car be immune from the competitive spirit that has driven men on throughout evolution? And if, as Irish freethinker George Bernard Shaw said, "All progress is the result of the efforts of unreasonable men", it should be no surprise that the new sport was quickly filled with such individuals. Some of them drove, where the core skill was in balancing grip in the corners against the engine's power; others concentrated on providing these daring men with ever-more grip, ever-more power. That was the essence of the very first auto race in 1895 and of every race thereafter.

Only the unreasonable engineer would be impatient with the performance of the ultimate speed machines he'd created and want still more, always more. The men sat in the cockpits needed to be unreasonable too, especially in the early days. The reasonable man would assess his chances of long-term survival as slim; the unreasonable man would absolutely assume that fate's fickle finger would tap only on the shoulders of others.

Besides, inside the car, the world beyond the driver's immediate horizon ceases to exist. Alone with the solitude of his desire, survival senses numbed by the speed, he's outrun the mediocrity of the outside world, slipped the shackles it tries to clamp on us all. He exists in a different place, some narrow-gauge aluminium tubing and a thin veneer of glass fibre all the physical reassurance of invulnerability he needs. He is running free, chased only by a fear

of failure, for failure is to risk ejection into the real world. "Racing is life," said Behra. "Everything else is just waiting." If that sounds like a drug addict desperate for his fix, the parallel is not without merit.

Even the bystander – the more reasonable man perhaps – feels the magnetic draw, whiffs the danger. He is mesmerised by the epic scale of the machine's performance and the jaw-dropping enormity of the driver's arrogance in assuming he can hang on to it, let alone exploit it, and still escape with his life. What to the driver is pure solitude and focus appears from the outside an uncontrollable, crazy blur of power, colour and noise that overwhelms the senses. The contrast in perspectives makes Einstein's relativity of time almost touchable: the Maserati speeds by, surging over a ribbon of asphalt through golden fields of wheat, a beautiful multi-cylinder wail trailing in its wake as the onlooker gathers his breath.

Who wouldn't be impressed by these matadors of speed in the early days of the F1 world championship as they tried to tame snarling, animalistic cars that would surely try to devour them – if the unyielding scenery didn't swallow them first?

But the world changes and F1 doesn't exist in a vacuum. As science took a proper hold on the design of the cars in the 1960s, the snarling animals morphed into true machines: featureless, cigar-shaped things – less beautiful, more purposeful, targeted and precise. But no less lethal. As such, the drivers evolved from matadors into test pilots. But still the essence of the sport – if something so complex as F1 can be described as a mere sport –

remained: hands on steering, feet on pedals, trading grip against power, fear of failure increasing the clamour for ever-more grip, ever-more power.

The aggregate result of all that striving for grip and power altered the fundamental perception of the sport's nature. The cars grew appendages that nailed them to the ground at previously undreamed cornering speeds and the form of their bodies became subservient to the function of airflow over these appendages. A Darwinian evolution of sorts could be discerned as its intricate specialisation pushed the racing car further apart from its road-going cousin. Because of the scale of performance of these machines and a nascent awareness of safety, the venues they raced at also had to change: no longer asphalt ribbons through fields of wheat or ancient Mediterranean towns and cities, but tracks purpose built to contain the spectacle.

In protecting the unreasonable men with a pathological fear of failure from themselves, the sport lost some of its epic and romantic qualities. But that's a perspective from the outside. From inside the car, with only the reassuring scream of an engine for company, the driver's absolute focus remained on exploiting that grip and power better than his rivals, better than he had ever done before, lest that chasing spectre caught him. That preoccupation filled his entire being; the backdrop was of no relevance.

Some rare men could see both sides. Jackie Stewart was one. When not racing, his unreasonable behaviour would be tucked

away safely in a metaphorical box, a facility that allowed him to see all too clearly motor racing within its true context. It was he, initially alone among his peers, who recognised the barbaric element of the sport and how it could not be allowed to be so in the changing world. His safety campaign began as a crusade but was soon encompassed by the mainstream, a process greased by the unstoppable tide of commercial sponsorship: blood and death sent out all the wrong messages for the marketeers selling product. And so the sport became squeezed into a philosophically smaller field of endeavour. In the 1930s Ernest Hemingway said there were only two sports: bullfighting and motor racing. You sense he wouldn't have approved of the direction the modern world imposed upon F1.

Still the competitors paid little heed. The junkies inside the cars pressed on, throttle wide open, brain tight shut. The junkies providing them with the machinery delighted in the cash the outside world's corporations were providing, so allowing them to make yet more specialised, marginalised machines that went yet faster. Ground effect chassis, turbocharged engines, super-sticky tyres, wind tunnels, test beds, materials technologists, software programs for computerised cars. The narrower the path that commerce and society obliged racing to take, the more intricate the solutions the junkies came up with in their never-ending fight against failure.

While the wider-sense challenge for today's F1 driver is certainly less than for his 1950s counterpart, paradoxically, it's more physically difficult. The penalty for getting it wrong is invariably less, but getting it right requires just as much feel and balance as well as rather more aggression. With 5g braking and 3g cornering forces and three times the power-to-weight ratio of Behra's Maserati, the window of opportunity for the correct inputs is vastly smaller than it was. But the environment in which today's cars are used allows drivers to exploit this window far more thoroughly than all but the grandmasters could hope to do back when it was more about adapting to a car's vices than exploiting its virtues.

For the designer and engineer, the challenge has changed from unlimited scope but limited resources to the absolute opposite. Ongoing legislation to control speeds has made the modern technical rule book so dense as to largely define the car's general layout. The challenge has shifted from chasing the limits of the universe to discovering and chasing ever-more microscopic layers of advantage: from Newtonian physics to quantum. Where the advantage comes from the junkies don't care – just keep it coming.

F1 has its own heartbeat. Commerce may use it and society may need to be protected from its excesses, but because it's junkie-driven, its life force is relentless. Outside factors merely determine its direction. For those who get inside its skin, its fascination remains undimmed. More grip, more power, more speed – suck in whatever the environment offers to keep that spectre off your back.

LEFT: Practice at the Nürburgring in 1968. Jack Brabham prepares to tackle 14 miles of high-speed crests, dives and blind corners – in nightmarish weather. He sits surrounded by fuel, his eponymous BT26 pushed on by 400 horsepower, with newfangled wings directing unknown forces through its suspension. The official is having second thoughts about allowing him out; only the true speed addict would query his hesitation. Brabham qualified 15th and finished fifth, ending a run of seven straight retirements.

TOP RIGHT: Brabham's Cooper T53 presses on between the lampposts and tramlines of the road circuit in Oporto. His victory in the 1960 Portuguese Grand Prix was his fifth in a row, and with it he secured his second consecutive world championship. He had, however, crashed out of the corresponding event the previous year when it was held in Lisbon's Monsanto Park. While attempting to lap a backmarker, Brabham's Cooper left the road and flattened a telegraph pole, knocking out the local phone service.

BOTTOM RIGHT: Privateer Ian Burgess rounds the Nürburgring's famous Karussell corner in his Anglo American Equipe-run Cooper T53. He would finish 11th in the 1962 German Grand Prix. This concrete banking was built in response to drivers continually hooking their inside-front wheels into the ditch.

PREVIOUS SPREAD:

TOP LEFT: Lotus boss Colin Chapman rests against the legend of Ferrari, the marque whose achievements he aspired to. These two teams would between them dominate F1 through the 1960s and '70s.

BOTTOM LEFT: Rain hit the Eifel mountains on the eve of the 1962 German Grand Prix. Here pole position man Dan Gurney gets his silver Porsche 804 away in the lead from Graham Hill's BRM P57 and John Surtees's Lola Mk4. Jim Clark's Lotus 25 is at the back, its driver having forgotten to switch on the fuel pump. This mistake set the scene for a great comeback drive from Clark, though Hill won the race from Surtees and Gurney.

RIGHT: As the 1950s gave way to the '60s, slimline machines of science like Brabham's Cooper T51 were fast taking over from the front-engined dinosaurs, and drivers faced a revised set of demands. Brabham, who is seen here in 1959, the year of his first world title, learned his craft in the rough, tough racing world of the Down Under dirt tracks and was easily recognisable because of his hunched driving position. His rivals half-jokingly said that he took a different racing line every lap – and were positively adamant that he never looked in his mirrors. A formidable opponent.

FAR LEFT: Fans at the 1964 Italian Grand Prix find a good, albeit dangerous, vantage point. At this stage F1 sponsorship was limited to trade suppliers such as motor oil, as shown here, and their wares were advertised only by the side of the tracks. Advertising on the cars was extremely restricted by the sporting regulations of the time, something that stretched back to the ethics of Grand Prix racing when it was conceived in the early 1900s. The time was fast approaching, however, when the commercial world would impose itself more aggressively on the sport.

LEFT: Smoke billows from the scene of Lorenzo Bandini's fatal accident at the 1967 Monaco Grand Prix. His Ferrari 312 crashed at The Chicane, a fast left-right flick that brought the cars back onto the harbour front.

RIGHT: The incomparable Jim Clark gives a two-fingered salute to his photographer friend David Phipps. During a lethal period of the sport Clark's continued mastery gave a false idea to some that so long as they were good enough, they would stay alive. Clark's death in 1968 shattered this illusion, removing his contemporaries' comfort blanket and leaving them feeling nakedly vulnerable.

LEFT: Jackie Stewart has just scored his 26th Grand Prix victory, beating the all-time record of his late friend Jim Clark. But the celebrations at the 1973 Dutch Grand Prix are muted because another of Stewart's colleagues, Roger Williamson, in only his second Grand Prix, has lost his life. Partly because of this depressing toll, Stewart had already decided that he would retire at the end of the year. But yet another driver would be killed before that time came: his Tyrrell team-mate, François Cevert. The mercurial Frenchman (in light blue overalls) joins Stewart having scored his fifth second place of the season.

TOP RIGHT: The Ferrari 312B2 of Jacky Ickx sits on the weighbridge in Brazil, 1973. The governing body had introduced a minimum weight in 1961 to counter the move of some makers towards ever-lighter and frailer machines. Stipulating a minimum weight is also a useful way of controlling straight-line speed, which is largely determined by the power-to-weight ratio. At the time of this photo the minimum was 575kg, though the technology of the time meant few teams would have been able to get below this even if they'd been allowed to. In the early 1980s creative interpretation of the regulation allowed certain British teams to run considerably lighter than the governing body had intended them to. This was a key bone of contention in the FISA/FOCA war.

BOTTOM RIGHT: A mechanic's witty reminder to James Hunt that his McLaren M23 has been fitted with new brake pads that will have to be bedded-in gently before he really goes for it.

With the lakes from which the Interlagos circuit takes its name in the background, Gilles Villeneuve's Ferrari 312T5 leads the first lap of the 1980 Brazilian Grand Prix. Following him are Didier Pironi's Ligier JS11/15, Jean-Pierre Jabouille's Renault RE20 and the Ligier of Jacques Laffite (Jabouille's brother-in-law and former mechanic). Jabouille had argued with Renault team manager Gérard Larrousse before the race about which car he had been assigned. His race chassis had suffered a turbo failure in the warm-up session, and because no cause had been established for this he wanted to race the spare car. Larrousse overruled him. Jabouille passed Pironi and Villeneuve and was comfortably in the lead on lap 26 when he suffered another turbo failure, handing the victory to team-mate René Arnoux (in fifth place here). It later emerged the failures had been caused by partially blocked oil pipes.

Alan Jones (in seventh place here) had been well below par in qualifying, the result of partying too hard before the race weekend. He made a vow never to repeat this mistake.

Running 15th in this photo is two-time world champion Emerson Fittipaldi in his self-built Fittipaldi F7. Later in the race his pride took a knock when he was overtaken by his junior team-mate – and future world champion – Keke Rosberg in a very marginal manoeuvre. Fittipaldi took umbrage and demanded that Rosberg be sacked. But his brother Wilson, who also happened to be his team manager, calmed the situation – and retained Rosberg. This would be Emerson's last season in F1 as a driver. He would, though, continue to run the team until it went bust at the end of 1982.

LEFT: **Certain personalities capture the public's imagination and briefly transcend the sport. Nigel Mansell did exactly that in the early 1990s, particularly in his British homeland. Within the sport, his skills weren't initially as widely appreciated. A hugely complex character, he used both the public's adoration and the F1 inner circle's ambivalence to fuel some of the most exciting, adrenaline-soaked performances the sport has ever seen. In this case, the public arguably got it more right than the cognoscenti.**

TOP RIGHT: **Other venues, such as Detroit (where Alain Prost is preparing to climb aboard his McLaren), have tried to copy the Monte Carlo blueprint of F1 cars racing through their streets, but without success.**

BOTTOM RIGHT: **Monte Carlo's impossibly glamorous backdrop fits so well with F1's self-image that its inclusion in the calendar is a given, even though its absurdly cramped street circuit was considered too tight for the much narrower and slower Grand Prix cars of the inaugural race there in 1929.**

LEFT: Ayrton Senna scored 35 of his 41 Grand Prix victories with McLaren. The other six were gleaned during his three-year spell at Lotus, 1985-87. He is seen here at Monza in 1988, the year he collected the first of his three world titles. This GP was memorable in that it was the only one of the 16-race season that McLaren didn't win. Senna was leading when he tripped over backmarker Jean-Louis Schlesser. The latter was in his only F1 race, deputising for an injured Nigel Mansell at Williams.

RIGHT: Not only did Senna end his F1 career at the wheel of a Williams, he began it the same way. As a fresh-faced F3 driver in 1983, the year he won the British title with the West Surrey Racing team, he tested for Frank Williams at Donington Park. McLaren also gave him a test, at Silverstone. He was impressive on both occasions, but would begin his F1 race career the following season with the lowly Toleman team.

Ayrton Senna, arguably the greatest driver of the modern era, in arguably its greatest car, the McLaren MP4/4-Honda, at Montreal in 1988. McLaren boss Ron Dennis brought together the ultimate 'dream team' by signing Senna to drive alongside the incumbent Alain Prost. Here were the two best racing drivers in the world, in the fastest car, with no team orders. Two thrilling, often controversial seasons were the upshot. Senna made it his mission to not only beat Prost but to do so by the maximum margin possible. Here in Canada the two were locked in battle right from the start. Prost led initially but was passed by Senna after being baulked by a backmarker. Prost fought back and both drivers set such a hot pace that the team was seriously concerned they were going to run out of fuel. This was at the time of the 150-litre fuel restriction and the telemetry from each car was showing that both cars were well 'in the red'. Prost set a new record on lap 45 (1min 25.3sec) and broke it on the very next lap (1min 25sec), a time that Senna promptly matched. At this stage McLaren imposed team orders so that a more economic pace could be set. Both drivers were told to reduce turbo boost pressure and retain positions. Only after Prost complied did Senna do likewise – and even then he insisted on having the last word, a 1min 24.97sec lap, before backing off and cruising to victory. The intensity of their personal rivalry had to be controlled by their team at times.

TOP LEFT: Yes, Monte Carlo is glamorous, but, more than at any other GP venue, there's an aspect of the flea circus to the driver's role as he sweats and strains to perform his perilous acrobatics for the amusement of the vaguely attentive onlookers.

BOTTOM LEFT: Michael Schumacher controls almost 800 horsepower as he threads his Ferrari F399 through the narrow Monaco streets in 1999. He would go on to score his fourth win at the world's most prestigious Grand Prix venue.

RIGHT: Seven world titles into his career, and by the end of 2004 the oldest man on the starting grid, Schumacher continues to provide F1's benchmark. How could an addict give this up? His only real competition has become time itself and the shadows it eventually casts.

Michael Schumacher struggled with the Ferrari F310B at the 1997 Italian Grand Prix, qualifying ninth and finishing sixth. Even the greatest driver of an era can't always transcend the limitations of his machinery. With a higher centre of gravity than the best of its rivals, this car tended to be hard on its tyres, a problem that proved particularly acute at Monza. The F310B was designed under the direction of John Barnard before his contract with the team came to an end early in 1997. His replacement, Rory Byrne, took over responsibility for the car: "I didn't really fully understand the car or the thought processes that had created it. We suffered a suspension failure early in testing and I wanted to take a look at the design loadings on the suspension – but there were no figures for it at the factory. It was John's design and he had taken all that information with him. I placed calls to him – but he didn't respond. It wasn't a bad car, but it's very difficult taking over someone else's design." So there you have it: F1 designers are every bit as competitive as F1 drivers.

LEFT: In a sport that is all about speed, here is F1's slowest corner, the hairpin at Monte Carlo, taken at around 30mph. Steering mechanisms have to be altered to provide enough lock to get round it without resorting to a three-point turn. This piece of Tarmac more usually plays host to the queuing traffic of aged millionaires exhausted after a day's shopping. But it also used to be the site of Monaco's railway station, a handsome building that was knocked down in the 1960s to make way for a hotel that has little to commend it, from the outside at least.

RIGHT: In 1998 McLaren provided Mika Häkkinen and David Coulthard with the fastest car in the field. They made good use of it, scoring five 1-2s. Häkkinen emerged as world champion after a close battle with Ferrari's Michael Schumacher. The Finn was generally reckoned to be the only driver that Schuey truly respected; this was a rivalry that stretched back to their F3 days of 1990. Coulthard, despite many fine performances, came to be locked into a supporting role to Häkkinen – and to his replacement, another Finn, Kimi Raikkonen.

LEFT: As an illustration of the staggering advances made in driver safety over the years, this incident at the 2002 Austrian Grand Prix was deeply impressive. Takuma Sato's Jordan has just taken a side-on hit from the Sauber of Nick Heidfeld. On tyres that had dropped out of their operating temperature window on account of a safety car period, Heidfeld lost control over a bump in the braking area. His car spun onto the infield grass at high speed, shot across the bows of the Williams of Juan Pablo Montoya (extreme left) and into the hapless Sato. In the years before compulsory tests that included side impacts, this would probably have proved fatal. Amazingly, Sato sustained only bruising; Heidfeld was unhurt.

TOP RIGHT: In the search for speed, big radiators cost aerodynamic performance. So radiators have become smaller. But smaller radiators mean insufficient cooling when the car is stationary on the grid. Which is why mechanics pack their intakes with dry ice.

BOTTOM RIGHT: F1 steering wheels are no longer merely for left and right – they house controls for varying the behaviour of sundry electronic performance aids, in an attempt to extract the maximum from the car over varying stages of fuel load, tyre wear and track conditions. Packed with so much technology, it's little wonder that they cost more than £10,000.

ABOVE AND RIGHT: With every participating speed-junkie squad straining to extremes to squeeze every possible atom of performance from packages that are tightly constrained by rigorous technical regulations, on-track performance has become more than ever defined by a team's resources. And Ferrari has the most to draw on. The cachet of its name, the symbiotic jet set glamour of its road cars, the direct link to its glorious and romantic history, its individuality as a Latin operative in a field of Anglo-Saxons – all these factors have been parlayed into income and political power. It used to be that the Scuderia dramatically underused these assets amid internal fighting, but latterly it has had discipline imposed from within. It used to be that the British teams would harness technical ingenuity to overcome Ferrari's in-built advantages, but latterly their scope for doing so has been all but squeezed dry by a tome of a rule book – some of which has been written as a direct result of Ferrari's influence – and by the fact that Ferrari now has a technical core at least as ingenious, an international broth of talent drawn from many of those other teams and moulded into a fighting unit. Business analysts tell us that a sponsorship association with Ferrari is worth approximately 40 per cent more than with any other F1 team – and so the spiral of its success continues, amplified by the skill of the world's best driver: Michael Schumacher. Meantime, its dominance is worrying to those looking at the sport's bigger picture.

Bloody Heroes

The Nürburgring, a 14-mile terror ride through Germany's Adenau forest, still stands as the most hellishly difficult racetrack man has ever devised. From the car, one blind brow looks much like any other, a critical horizon where the green of this world meets the blue of eternity. In 1957, 46-year-old Juan Manuel Fangio clinched his fifth world title there with a drive so staggering that it verges on mystical.

Recovering from a badly botched pit stop by his Maserati mechanics that left him almost 50 seconds behind the Ferraris of Mike Hawthorn and Peter Collins, Fangio clawed it all back in eight laps, passed them and won. A man needs to reach deep, deep within himself to go eight seconds per lap faster than his own pole position time. In the biography Fangio by Roberto Carozzo, he recalled that comeback: "I came to the dip below the bridge… This time I didn't lift my foot off the accelerator. Normally we took that curve in fifth [gear], trying to skim rather than jump, so as not to jolt the car and allow a margin for error when it landed. This time I took it without slackening at all, with my foot down. I tried to stick well to the inside of the dip, where the car took off, and I touched the ground on the opposite side of the track, uncomfortably close to the fence. There were no guard rails in those days. In my mirror I saw the cloud of dust I'd raised at the edge of the racetrack. It was a risk worth taking. The curve linked the two straights and I had treated it as if it were just one straight. I knew I'd made up some seconds there."

Today, a driver who tries to push through a corner harder than he's ever pushed before usually risks no more than a trip through a gravel trap. Furthermore, even if he hits something solid, he is strapped tight within a carbon fibre tub of immense strength that has passed incredibly rigorous crash tests before even being allowed onto a track. When Fangio assessed in that split second whether he could keep his foot flat to the floor instead of lifting, in judging whether that would take him to the dusty edge of the grass or beyond, the trip he risked wasn't through a gravel trap, it was to the morgue. He made hundreds of such decisions every lap. That is the fundamental difference between the challenge then and the challenge now.

A 1950s driver had to gauge the level of his ability and drive to it. Those who didn't, who pressed on until they found their limits, tended not to survive. Fangio, on that August afternoon in 1957, surrendered his normal discipline and ate into his survival reserves. As his adrenaline levels dipped, he became only too aware of this: "That day I was ready to do anything. When it was all over I was convinced I would never be able to drive like that again – ever. I had reached the limit of my concentration and will to win… I knew I could win, but I knew equally I could lose." And he wasn't referring merely to the race.

It was this raw, unsanitised environment that made the sport's essence so much more visible than it later became. Played out

Hans Herrmann flips his British Racing Partnership-run BRM P25 at the 1959 German Grand Prix. Given the lack of roll-over protection in the cars of the day, he is no doubt thanking his lucky stars there were no seat belts to retain him. Remarkably, the German suffered no serious injuries. This race was held at the Avus circuit, basically two 2.5-mile carriageways of a Berlin *autobahn* linked by this tight hairpin at its southern tip and a high brick banking to the north. This Grand Prix was unique in that it was purposely run over two heats, each of 30 laps; Tony Brooks won both of them, his American team-mates Dan Gurney and Phil Hill completing a Ferrari 1-2-3.

against backdrops dripping with sun-soaked romance – Monaco, Casablanca, Pescara – the contestants were cast in a truly heroic light, capturing the imagination in a way that would be impossible to replicate today. And when the afternoon's gladiatorial contest was over, the driver would wipe the grime from his face, light a cigarette and kiss the attractive woman, possibly an actress, standing adoringly by his side. Only then might he receive the news: another of his peers had set sail for Valhalla, the place of the fallen warriors. They would drink to his memory tonight.

Fifties Grand Prix racers Alberto Ascari, Erwin Bauer, Don Beauman, Jean Behra, Felice Bonetto, Ivor Bueb, Piero Carini, Eugenio Castellotti, Peter Collins, Luigi Fagioli, Joe Fry, Pierre 'Levegh', Stuart Lewis-Evans, Herbert Mackay-Fraser, Onofre Marimón, Luigi Musso, Alfonso de Portago, Louis Rosier, Archie Scott-Brown, Raymond Sommer, Charles de Tornaco, Ken Wharton, Peter Whitehead and Bill Whitehouse were all killed during the decade while racing or testing.

For men like Fangio, for many the greatest champion of them all, the brooding shadow that followed the sport imposed a deep spirituality. Ostensibly a quiet, humble man, he drew heavily on the human spirit but had a keen recognition of when to turn down invitations to indulge his talent. He was a tiger who hunted alone. For others, any foreboding seemed to bring them together and a heady social life formed around the Grand Prix scene, with young

Brits Collins and Hawthorn in its vanguard. Why not live life to the full when the next horizon, the next bend, could be the last?

Collins, good-looking, driving for Ferrari and married to a beautiful actress – all by his mid-20s – portrayed a devil-may-care image. But don't imagine there wasn't a cost. Team owner Ken Gregory shared a room with him on occasion: "Peter enjoyed every single moment of life. But I do wonder if there was some struggle going on inside. Sometimes he would scream out terribly in his sleep."

Team owner John Cooper recalled an incident at an infamous meeting place/watering hole in Reims, venue of the 1958 French Grand Prix: "It was the night before the race. There were two trees in the courtyard and after a few drinks Hawthorn and Lewis-Evans had a bet about which of them would be the first to get to the top of these trees. And so off they climbed. Then Stirling Moss, who was standing there, notices that there's water falling on him. He looks up and it's Hawthorn peeing on him. 'I've always wanted to piss on you from a great height, Moss!' he shouted."

The next day Musso – Ferrari team-mate to Hawthorn and Collins – was killed attempting to take one of Reims' high-speed curves slightly too fast. The young Italian was even braver than he was talented, a lethal combination back then. It transpired he was desperate to win the race: he needed its prize money to pay off his gambling debts. Another live-fast, B-movie twist to the era's plot.

This close-knit community lost members with a sickening regularity. One year on, at the next Grand Prix get-together in Reims, those two carefree tree-climbers were just memories, their obituary pages already yellowing. Maybe the numbing scale of death in the recent Second World War made such things less shocking than they would be today. And amid the greyness of rationing and post-war austerity, these gladiators cast long, long shadows as they flew close to the flame.

A gathering of drivers from any era will include a variety of characters, but with its heroic, romantic setting and the cult of personality just beginning to take hold, their differences were somehow amplified in the 1950s. The inauguration of a drivers' world championship in 1950 contributed to this. There had been a world championship in the 1920s – but it had been for cars, not drivers. Whereas the spotlight had previously been shone on the machinery, the public could now pick out the light and shade of the men involved. These traits were seen as reflected in their qualities in battle.

The first world champion, Giuseppe Farina, was "a very proud man", says Moss. "He did not like to be beaten. This is an asset of all the top drivers, but it was particularly noticeable in him. On a good day he could push Fangio or Ascari, but I don't think it came as easily. He was a very hard fighter but it could extend to pulling some tricks on the track that were not really acceptable. He could

play very dirty." Two pre-war Grand Prix drivers – Marcel Lehoux and Laszlo Hartmann – literally did not survive on-track skirmishes with the Italian, and the power that brought to his presence in a rival's mirrors can only be imagined.

In contrast, Moss idolises Fangio – world champion of 1951 and 1954-57: "If you're talking single-seaters, he was the best in the world, I believe the best there's ever been: enormous talent, stamina, great concentration, very easy on the vehicle. Because he was so good he would get the best contracts and cars, which was part of it. But he got the best cars because he was the best damn driver, and that compounded the problem of trying to beat him. I don't really know if he was a fighter because he didn't need to very often. But I suppose his fabulous drive at the Nürburgring in 1957 showed that he was if needed."

Alberto Ascari, dominant champion in 1952 and '53, had a beautiful driving style that belied his furious speed. Enzo Ferrari considered him "virtually unbeatable" if he hit the front, but he showed rather more frailty when in any other position. His fights were with demons rather than other drivers. He was a man obsessed with fate and numerology. His father, the great Antonio Ascari, was killed while leading the 1925 French Grand Prix – when Alberto was not quite seven. By 1955 Alberto was approaching the age his father had been at the time of his death; he became

preoccupied with that coming milestone. Just one day short of it, he crashed into the harbour during the Monaco Grand Prix – but escaped with cuts and bruises. Two days later, amid great relief, he exceeded his father's age. Two days after that, this 'Man with Two Shadows' was killed in a mysterious testing accident. "There was virtually no difference between Ascari and Fangio in speed," says Moss, "but Alberto was *definitely* not a fighter."

Not like Jean Behra. Not as touched by the angels as Ascari, the Frenchman was above all else a scrapper who seemed to delight in his underdog status, particularly when he drove for the underfunded French Gordini team. Behra was Moss's 1956 Maserati team-mate: "A tough guy. He was very tenacious. If you passed him you couldn't just forget about him – he'd come back at you. He was very competitive, in the way that Jack Brabham was later. He wasn't as quick as someone like Tony Brooks, but he was quick enough and combative enough to give you bother. Even if you felt you could beat him, he often made you work a damn sight harder than you might have expected."

In 1959 Behra was paired with Brooks at Ferrari and was taken aback by his team-mate's speed. His driving acquired a desperate edge, something that led indirectly to his dismissal from the team. Four weeks later Behra was killed in a sports car race.

Mike Hawthorn became Britain's first world champion when he narrowly – not from a great height, as he'd shouted from up his tree – beat Moss to the 1958 title. He immediately retired, only to perish in a road accident a few months later. "Mike could be a terrific competitor," says Moss, "but I don't think his pure ability was up with the very top guys. When he was having a good day he was a factor, but he was a bit inconsistent – whether that was because of his health, which wasn't very good, I'm not qualified to say. When you passed him you didn't usually have much to worry about afterward. I'd put him marginally ahead of Peter Collins, though. Peter was more consistent, without reaching the same heights Mike did on his good days; he was really pretty good but never did anything sensational, never did a Nürburgring '57."

If the Battle of Britain spirit of a young fighter pilot – almost certainly aware of his imminent doom and covering his fear with high-spirited, hedonistic dash – was present in any of the drivers, it was in Hawthorn. The melancholy became more visible in the last few months of his career – ironically his title-winning campaign – and the likely reason wasn't hard to fathom. He had watched in horror as his close friend, party ally and team-mate Collins crashed fatally right in front of him during the German Grand Prix. His mate had probably been overreaching himself, eating into those survival margins, in trying to stay with the sublimely gifted Brooks.

FAR LEFT: **Stirling Moss drives the Vanwall to victory in the 1957 British Grand Prix at Aintree: the first world championship win for a British driver in a British car. In fact, there were two British drivers involved, for Moss took over Tony Brooks's car after his own suffered engine problems. Brooks wasn't yet fully fit after an accident in the previous month's Le Mans sports car race where he'd been pinned beneath his rolled Aston Martin. His first time behind the wheel since then had been when he'd driven his road car to Aintree for this race.**

LEFT: **Alberto Ascari's Ferrari 500 in the process of dominating the 1953 British Grand Prix. During 1952-53 Ascari won a remarkable nine consecutive Grands Prix, a record that still stands. The Ferrari 500 won 14 races in a row, also providing outright victories for Piero Taruffi, Giuseppe Farina and Mike Hawthorn.**

The latter was a driver whose rare intelligence was exceeded only by his natural talent. Although of the same generation and nationality, he shunned the excesses of Hawthorn and Collins. All too aware of the dangerous places that desperation could draw you to, he had a shrewd feel for just how high his limitations were. And when circumstances allowed, he exercised that skill with clinical precision and discipline. But he was never, ever, consumed by desire. By his standards, even Fangio indulged himself occasionally. Brooks's drives were demonstrations of an art form that could reduce the opposition to background detail. "To fight at all costs back then was, in my opinion, to invite the men in white coats to take you into protective custody," he says today.

Brooks never won the world championship but came close to doing so in 1959. At the start of the final round he was hit from behind by a team-mate on the first lap. Rather than race on regardless, his sanity compelled him to pit for a damage check. There was no damage. And no title. But he's still alive.

"Tony Brooks is the greatest 'unknown' driver there has ever been," says Moss. "There's no one else as good who is so little known. But those of us inside the sport know how brilliant he was. There are many drivers who are household names that simply weren't in the same class. He had a fantastic talent. You saw that at the circuits that demanded ability above all else: the old Spa and the old Nürburgring.

He wasn't a fighter particularly, he just isn't that sort of man; he's an introvert. I'm not that way and I *needed* to race. I don't think Tony ever had that need. He was probably smarter in his approach than I was. He could sit back and let it all unfold, whereas I had to be in there, fighting. I think, like me, he kept something in reserve for error or mischance. Someone like Lewis-Evans drove faster, I think, than he should have done, whereas Tony wouldn't."

Of course, Brooks wasn't the only giant of this era never to win the F1 title. Moss didn't either, even though there was unanimous agreement among his peers of the period 1958-61 that he was the greatest of them all. As gifted as Brooks but with an overwhelming competitive urge, Moss had no room for Hawthorn's or Collins's casual use of talent. In its place was relentless application. "Stirling was the very first motor racing professional in the modern sense," says his then-manager Ken Gregory. "He was absolutely committed to racing. By any measure he was a clinical, cold professional, a bit like Michael Schumacher today – but with a better temperament. He'd smoke, but no more than four or five a day; he didn't drink; he wouldn't have sex on a race weekend."

Better still, Moss tried not to dwell on what he was doing, saying to his biographer: "When I go to bed, I hope to be tired, very tired, because I don't want to think."

Or wake up screaming.

OPPOSITE: **Moss greets Juan Manuel Fangio, the man he considered the master of Grand Prix driving. During their season together at Mercedes-Benz in 1955, Moss would follow Fangio closely – so closely that they were called 'The Train' – and, from the best seat in the house, enjoy an F1 masterclass. He learned well. Following Fangio's retirement in 1958, Moss was held in similar awe by his peers.**

The start of the Silverstone
Formula Libre race held just hours
after the 1953 British Grand Prix.
Mike Hawthorn's 2.5-litre Ferrari
(far right) gets the drop on Juan
Manuel Fangio's BRM V16 (far left).
The car next to Fangio's is Giuseppe
Farina's Thinwall Special. There is a
strong link between the three –
BRM, Thinwall Special and Ferrari.
Tony Vandervell held the patent
for the Thinwall bearing that was
a major breakthrough in aircraft
and automotive engine efficiency.
A wealthy British industrialist, he
had been a major contributor to
the BRM project, a trust set up to
design and build a car that would
take on the world in F1 and thereby
advertise post-war Britain's
technological excellence. But he
left in disgust because of what he
saw as inept management and
instead cajoled Enzo Ferrari into
supplying him with F1 cars, which
Vandervell then had modified into
Thinwall Specials. This particular
version was based on the Ferrari
375, the type that had won the
1951 Grand Prix at this same circuit.
This was the established pacesetter
that the BRM V16 would have gone
head to head with in 1952 had it
been ready in time. As it was, with
no effective opposition – Alfa
Romeo had withdrawn – facing
Ferrari, the governing body decided
to run Grands Prix under the 2-litre
Formula Two regulations. Ferrari
still cleaned up, but at least the
grids were fuller. This Libre race,
however, showed what might have
been. In winning it Farina recorded
the first official 100mph lap of the
track. In contrast, the Grand Prix's
fastest lap was 95.790mph, set by
José Froilán González's Maserati
A6GCM. There had been another
change of formula – to 2.5 litres –
by the time the Thinwall Specials
had morphed into the famous
teardrop Vanwalls of Stirling Moss
and Tony Brooks. It was with these
machines, by now totally unrelated
to Ferrari, that Vandervell finally
beat "the bloody red cars". Ill
health forced him to drastically
cut back his involvement in the
sport after 1958.

Juan Manuel Fangio in the BRM
V16 during the 1953 Formula Libre
race at Silverstone. He finished
second behind the Thinwall Special
of Giuseppe Farina. The BRM was
such a fantastically complicated
beast that by the time its
hard-pressed team had finally got
it running properly it was no longer
eligible for world championship
races. Its best performance in a
Grand Prix proper was Reg Parnell's
fifth place in the 1951 British Grand
Prix. He finished five laps behind
the winning Ferrari, and in agony
because the car's fierce cockpit
temperature had burned his feet.

TOP RIGHT: **Stirling Moss** after winning the 1959 Portuguese Grand Prix at Monsanto by more than a lap. At the peak of his form, Moss qualified over two seconds faster around this Lisbon parkland track than Jack Brabham's similar Cooper-Climax and led the race from start to finish. Brabham crashed out and it was left to his American team-mate Masten Gregory to give forlorn chase to Moss.

BOTTOM RIGHT: **Piero Taruffi, Giuseppe Farina and Alberto Ascari**, three Italians all driving for Ferrari, discuss tactics before the 1953 British Grand Prix. Enzo Ferrari became rather less patriotic in his choice of drivers during the later 1950s. He reasoned that he didn't get such a hard time from his local press in the event of a fatality if the driver involved wasn't Italian.

FAR LEFT: José Froilán González has the faraway look of a warrior about to do battle. Drivers of the early 1950s tended to wear a visor in wet conditions, and many kept a spare pair of goggles around their neck.

LEFT: Once Alberto Ascari has put his gloves on he is fully kitted-up, 1950s-style. Flame-proof overalls unheard of, seat belts considered dangerous – just a red Ferrari to drive, with a clear track in front of him.

RIGHT: Peter Collins seemingly had it all: talent, youth, looks, beautiful wife. But Enzo Ferrari perhaps disturbed his equilibrium when he suggested that marriage had taken the edge off his speed. Suddenly, Collins became a tiger in the car; his victory in the 1958 British Grand Prix transcended his previous performances. But two weeks later he was killed at the Nürburgring, arguably driving beyond his natural level – a lethal game to play in the F1 of the time.

FOLLOWING SPREAD:
LEFT: Giuseppe Farina was a proud racer who would sometimes resort to unacceptably dangerous tactics in the heat of battle. He continued in F1 until 1955 when in his late-40s. A sports car crash had left him with badly burned legs and he needed morphine to complete that year's scorching-hot Argentinian Grand Prix. He was killed in a road accident in 1966 while on his way to spectate at the French Grand Prix. Juan Manuel Fangio, his one-time team-mate, had long warned him that he relied too much on his guardian angel when driving on the open road.

RIGHT: Stirling Moss served part of his Grand Prix apprenticeship in the outclassed HWM. He is being push-started by the Walton-on-Thames team's founders, John Heath (nearest camera) and George Abecassis (behind Moss's helmet).

Get the Drift

Behind the deeds of the heroes of the 1950s there was technique. The skills required of a racing driver haven't really altered since the sport was invented: he needs to feel the car's messages through his hands and posterior, needs the hand-to-eye co-ordination to make the right reactions to those messages, needs an acute inner ear feel for changes in lateral force through a corner. But the way in which these skills are expressed has been dictated by the cars. The front-engine car of the 1950s required a fundamentally different technique to what followed. It was all about high-speed drift.

The physics of a high-powered car on skinny tyres, with its engine up front, were about momentum rather than quick direction changes. A car with plenty of weight at its extremities – engine one end, gearbox and differential the other – and not much between means that it has a high polar moment of inertia, i.e. it changes direction gradually but the direction-change, once made, carries a lot of momentum. Imagine a heavy door with weights bolted to its outer edges; it would be difficult to push open, but, once you'd got the initial movement, it would be difficult to stop, too.

The trick of the 1950s F1 designer was having that momentum carried more through the rear wheels than the front. If the front carried too much the car would understeer, i.e. would want to run straight on, and the driver would need to come off the power to utilise weight transference to restore front-end grip. Very time-consuming. If, on the other hand, the cornering momentum went more through the rear wheels the car would oversteer, i.e. turn more than it had initially been asked to, and, with some skill on the driver's part, skim through the turn at just the right angle. With low-grip tyres, the driver would use the throttle pedal to adjust the extent of this oversteer, modulating the power going through the rear wheels. This sapped far less momentum than having to make the big throttle lift-offs that were necessary to banish understeer.

This power drift made the cornering limit of the 1950s Grand Prix car an ill-defined, fuzzy thing. As that limit approached, the car replied only vaguely and with a delay to steering input, and in that nebulous area a great driver could weave his magic while the less-than-great would (hopefully) recognise their limitations. It was a door only a few could pass through.

"Yes, I guess it sorted out the men from the boys," says Tony Brooks, a master of the drift. "These cars were not what you would call manoeuvrable and they'd only really come into their own in high-speed corners, of which the tracks of the time had plenty. They didn't have a lot of pure roadholding and you felt that both in cornering and applying the power. Good throttle control and a feel and judgement for drift were essential.

Juan Manuel Fangio concentrates as he drifts his Lancia-Ferrari, only his uncanny feel and flawless technique preventing him from flying off the road into the unyielding scenery. This is at Silverstone's Copse Corner in 1956, the year of Fangio's only British Grand Prix victory.

FAR LEFT: Alberto Ascari, José Froilán González and Giuseppe Farina gather on the grid before the 1953 British Grand Prix at Silverstone. Ascari takes sustenance before going on to dominate the race. His Ferrari team-mate Farina would finish a subdued third, with González fourth in his Maserati after being black-flagged for spilling oil and pitting to remonstrate with the brave official.

LEFT: Luigi Musso (in fez) and Mike Hawthorn confer with Ferrari team manager Romolo Tavoni. Despite being Italian, Musso was the team outsider. He was killed at the 1958 French Grand Prix as he attempted to close down Hawthorn's lead.

"You would just turn into the corner and, if you'd judged your entry speed correctly, and the car was working well, the drift would begin. You would then just steer it on the throttle. It needed a delicate touch not to let the drift build into a big slide or to let the speed come down so low that you lost the drift. If you couldn't do that you weren't going to be quick, basically.

"Some cars just wouldn't allow you to drive like that – and they were bad cars. The 1956 BRM I drove was lethal – and I don't use that word lightly – precisely because it wouldn't drift. You had to corner that car absolutely geometrically; if you had the slightest deviation from that line it threw you off. I overturned one at the British Grand Prix when the throttle stuck open at a fast corner. Any other car would have just slid along the grass for a while then rejoined the track.

"The Maserati 250F was the best car for drifting. It was actually difficult *not* to drive it in drift. The Vanwall wasn't quite so easy in that it had higher limits but required a lot more precision to drift it successfully. It was faster but more demanding."

In this way F1 driving in extremis was a thing of very real, if transient, beauty – a beauty that was intensified by the price of getting it wrong.

If there was art in the driving, there was, too, in the construction of the cars that achieved this delicate balance. "It wasn't really science," says Brooks. "It was a bit hit and miss. They would try to ensure the chassis was as stiff as possible, then play with the springs, get the weight as low down as possible – but beyond that it was a black art really."

It was a craft that the Italians – Alfa Romeo, Maserati and Ferrari – had a great feel for, honed by decades of in-the-field experience. Later, more scientific designs from Mercedes-Benz and Vanwall should have shown a greater superiority over the Italians than they actually did. The fact that they did not generally drift as well is the only explanation for this disparity. Great care was taken with the Maserati 250F, for example, to minimise suspension geometry changes as it rolled under cornering load. In this way its driver could fully exploit the characteristics of the tyres of the time: they deformed progressively under load. They would produce their maximum tractive force when running at around 12 per cent of slip angle, i.e. the difference between the angle of the tyre's contact patch and the car's direction of travel. The driver would allow that angle of slip to build on the entry to a corner and then, just short of overstepping it, apply the power to maintain the angle. Any car that made it easier for him to maintain the desired slip angle had a hidden performance factor that couldn't be explained by its horsepower, drag co-efficient or chassis stiffness.

Art or science, it mattered little to the men inside them. Just keep it coming – more, always more.

OPPOSITE: Mike Hawthorn and Stirling Moss share a joke in the midst of their battle for the 1958 world championship. In contrast to some of the acrimonious title struggles in modern F1, Moss actually stood as Hawthorn's key witness when the latter appealed against disqualification from the Portuguese Grand Prix. Hawthorn won his appeal. Had he not done so, Moss would have taken the crown. As it was, Hawthorn did.

A significant moment in motorsport history unfolds at Silverstone in 1951. José Froilán González (12) gets his second Grand Prix with Ferrari under way, going neck and neck with Giuseppe Farina's Alfa Romeo (1) as Juan Manuel Fangio (2) lags behind his Alfa Romeo team-mate Felice Bonetto (4) and the Ferrari of Alberto Ascari (11). Fangio and González would stage a race-long battle well clear of the others, with the Ferrari driver eventually getting the upper hand, aided by his car's superior fuel consumption enabling him to run longer before refuelling. After 90 laps he crossed the finish line to record Ferrari's first world championship-status Grand Prix victory.

LEFT: Jack Brabham would never have gelled with Enzo Ferrari. Down-to-earth, tough and taciturn, he was his own boss even when ostensibly employed by Cooper, with whom he won the world championship in 1959 and 1960. By 1963 he'd left Cooper to found the Brabham team. When he won a third title in 1966 he became the only man to achieve this distinction while driving for his own team.

RIGHT: José Froilán González adjusts his goggles. Because of his new-boy status within Ferrari he had fully expected Alberto Ascari, the team's number one driver, to commandeer his car when he came into the pits for his refuelling stop at Silverstone in 1951; Ascari had retired his own machine with gearbox problems. As González pulled up he made to get out, only for Ascari to reassure him that it was okay to stay where he was.

BELOW: Extreme heat during the 1959 French Grand Prix at Reims melted the track's surface and caused many drivers to spin. Maurice Trintignant struggles to restart his Cooper T51 while the Ferrari 246 Dino of Jean Behra surges past. The latter had stalled at the start and was in the process of charging from dead last to fourth. His efforts came to naught, however, when he over-revved the engine. Tired and disappointed, he lost his temper when his team manager immediately took him to task. He knocked Romolo Tavoni to the ground with a single punch and, unsurprisingly, was dismissed from the team. Behra was killed four weeks later after crashing his own Porsche sports car in a minor race at Avus in Germany.

TOP RIGHT: Mike Hawthorn's Ferrari 246 Dino at Spa in the 1958 Belgian Grand Prix. He set pole position and finished second behind the Vanwall of Tony Brooks, a driver who was perhaps even better than Stirling Moss at this ultra-fast road circuit. Hawthorn backed off part-way through the race after seeing a wrecked Ferrari in a field and believing it was his friend, Peter Collins. In fact, it was that of Luigi Musso, who climbed out unhurt on this occasion. Within a few months, though, Hawthorn, Collins and Musso would be dead.

BOTTOM RIGHT: Karl Kling splashes around Silverstone in 1954 aboard the radical-looking Mercedes-Benz W196. There was no rule requiring F1 cars to have open wheels until 1961, though only a few designers had tried to take advantage of the lower drag resulting from enclosing them. There were downsides to doing so: as well as being heavier than the equivalent open-wheel version of the car, the W196 streamliner suffered an aerodynamically induced handling imbalance in fast corners.

King George VI is introduced to the drivers prior to the 1950 British Grand Prix, the inaugural race of the F1 world championship. To his left are princesses Elizabeth and Margaret. But they are not the only royalty present: the man in the far right of the picture is Prince Birabongse Bhanuban of Siam (now Thailand), a talented driver in his own right. Racing as 'B Bira', he was best of the rest this day behind the four dominant Alfa Romeos before retiring his Maserati 4CLT/48 with a fuel-feed problem. *This* day was a Saturday – a Silverstone tradition for decades – in order not to impinge upon the village's church service! An estimated crowd of 100,000 came to see the world's top drivers in action around the converted Bomber Command aerodrome in sleepy Northamptonshire. Despite the wartime hangover of petrol rationing, the surrounding roads were gridlocked on race morning. The venue was overwhelmed; gate personnel couldn't cope with the sheer numbers and many spectators were able to get in free – just like the royal family.

FAR LEFT: Juan Manuel Fangio prepares to do a few practice laps on the closed public roads of Rouen – venue of the 1957 French Grand Prix – in the car of Maserati team-mate and fellow countryman Carlos Menditéguy. As the team's lead driver, Fangio naturally got first choice of equipment. In stark contrast to the highly dedicated Fangio, Menditéguy was the archetypal playboy racer; he was said to be enjoying a liaison with Brigitte Bardot at this particular time. He complained that he seemed to be getting the worst of the team's cars. An amused Fangio replied: "What do you expect – the best ones?"

LEFT: That self-confessed "agitator of men" Enzo Ferrari (in braces) stirs things up during a test at Modena in 1958. Early the previous year Ferrari had asked that one of his drivers, Eugenio Castellotti, cut short his holiday with his fiancée, a famous singer, to attend a meaningless test at Modena. Rival Maserati had just broken the lap record there and Ferrari wanted it back. Furthermore, he believed that Castellotti's performances were being compromised by his current relationship. The driver's irritation was intensified when he arrived to find a steady drizzle falling. On his second lap he crashed, fatally.

1954 – NEW FORMULA

MAXIMUM ENGINE CAPACITY: 2.5 litres normally aspirated; 750cc with forced induction.

The Grand Prix car of this era was conceptually similar to what had been raced since the turn of the century. There had been vast improvements in technology during that time: engine efficiency had made great strides, suspension was more advanced, gearboxes had been improved and moved to the rear to even-up weight distribution. But not much had changed in overall layout and principle: the engine sat up front and drove through a propshaft to rear wheels that wore skinny tyres. The Maserati 250F was a typical example of the breed.

1954 MASERATI 250F (TOP LEFT)

LAYOUT: front-engined, rear-wheel drive, rear-mounted four-speed gearbox
CHASSIS: multi-tubular with bolted-on aluminium body panels, independent front suspension by wishbone links and coil springs, semi-independent rear suspension by de Dion tube and transverse leaf spring
BRAKES: hydraulically operated drum brakes front and rear
ENGINE: alloy-block 2.5-litre, six cylinders in-line, three carburettors, 240bhp @ 6500rpm
WEIGHT: 630kg

Radical changes to F1 design were just over the horizon, but before then came some significant detail developments.

MID-1954 – SPACE FRAME CONSTRUCTION, FUEL INJECTION & DISC BRAKES

The Mercedes-Benz W196 (top right), which made a winning debut in the French Grand Prix, utilised narrow-diameter tubes arranged and welded in such a way
that their geometry formed a structurally rigid whole, without the need for heavy bolstering ladder frames. It also featured fuel injection, which had first been used on World War Two aircraft engines; it kept their combustion consistent over a wider range of operating conditions.

Also developed in the aircraft industry, disc brakes were first used in a Grand Prix by the Vanwall Special at Silverstone. They improved

ultimate stopping power only slightly but were much more resistant to fade at high speed and provided greater consistency over a race distance. Just five years after the introduction of the Maserati 250F, the Grand Prix car had become an entirely different beast, built by a very different sort of team. A revolution had occurred, triggered by a left-field design from Cooper. This British constructor had been established in the early post-war years building cars for a new junior category called Formula Three (bottom left) – a name the sport's governing body adopted in 1950 – which catered for cheap 500cc cars. Motorbike engines were used and the logical place for them was behind the driver but just ahead of the axle line so that they could power the rear wheels via their usual chain-drive mechanism. This so-called mid-engine layout – any engine sited between the axles is mid-engined, no matter its relationship to the driver – had been tried in pre-war Grand Prix racing (in 1923 by Benz and throughout much of the 1930s by Auto Union) but not in such a way that its inherent dynamic advantages were exploited. These gradually became apparent to Cooper – and they took them right to the very top.

1958 – MID-MOUNTED ENGINE

Stirling Moss drove a Cooper T43 – a beefed-up F2 car – to a sensational victory in the season-opening Argentinian Grand Prix, defeating the proud thoroughbreds from Maserati and Ferrari. The revolution had threatened. Now it kicked off. Soon it would be in power.

A couple of years before his death in 2001, John Cooper recalled the development of the mid-engine theme: "Well, even when we went beyond Formula 500 we still liked the layout, principally because it was cheap: it meant you could make a very simple frame. But it wasn't until we built the bobtailed, mid-engined Cooper sports car in the mid-1950s that we thought we might be on to something. That was a super car: very light, very easy on its tyres, you sat low down – and it was very cheap. It just seemed so right. Then we built a single-seater version of that, and as soon as Coventry Climax developed a twin-cam version of its engine, we had something we could do something with. We'd entered Grands Prix before that, of course, but that was simply because the regulations allowed us to and

because there was some start money in it, not because we thought we had a chance.

"Having said all that, though, we were still, I think, as surprised as the other teams by that win in Argentina."

A reduction of Grand Prix distances as from 1958 – from approximately 300 miles to approximately 200 – also helped Cooper's cause. There was now no room for pit stops if you wanted to win: compact, light on fuel, light on tyres was the way to go.

In 1959 a further development of Cooper's mid-engined 'pioneer' (bottom right) won the world championship.

1959 COOPER T51

LAYOUT: mid-engined, rear-wheel drive, rear-mounted five-speed gearbox
CHASSIS: multi-tubular with bolted-on aluminium body panels, independent suspension front and rear via wishbone links and coil springs
BRAKES: hydraulically operated disc brakes front and rear
ENGINE: Coventry Climax 2.5-litre, four cylinders in-line, two carburettors, 240bhp @ 6750rpm
WEIGHT: 460kg

It wasn't only the design of the Cooper that was revolutionary. The way in which it was conceived and built – using bought-in engines and gearboxes from proprietary manufacturers and adapting parts from wherever they could be cheaply sourced – made F1 far more accessible to those heavy on ideas but light on resources. This ultimately took F1 away from the grip of road-car producers and led to a nucleus of specialist constructors – mainly British – operating along much the same principles as Cooper. This nucleus would dominate the sport for the next few decades.

From Matadors to Test Pilots

Stirling Moss's win with a tiny mid-engined Cooper in the 1958 Argentinian Grand Prix was the meteorite that killed the dinosaurs. That spindly machine is the ancestor of every successful Grand Prix car since.

Within 18 months mid-engined cars would reign supreme. This layout made for pared-down-to-essentials machines that lacked the visual majesty of their front-engined forebears. No longer snarling, animalistic monsters, just cool, featureless, cigar-shaped tubes on wheels. No more compound curves of hand-beaten aluminium to encompass distinct profile changes, instead just a flat, low-drag oneness. No longer a driver sitting on top of the car, trying to tame it. Instead, he lay within, almost prone, part of the car, not fighting it.

With no propshaft to clear, the driver could be positioned much closer to the ground and the car itself could be smaller. This reduced the frontal area by approximately 75 square centimetres over a front-engined equivalent; this alone equated to around 25 horse-power. The advantages snowballed: a smaller car is lighter, creates less drag, needs to carry around less fuel, which in turn makes it yet lighter. The torque reactions of engine and transaxle oppose each other. In a front-engined car the separate structures supporting each of these components had to be sturdy enough to absorb these forces. In a mid-engined car, with engine and transaxle at the same end and no propshaft running between them, the torque reactions cancelled each other out.

Critically, the mid-engined car's mass was centralised, lowering the polar moment of inertia, inducing the car to react more directly to steering input, making it more responsive and agile. Furthermore, the reduced weight asked less of the tyres. The 1959 Cooper weighed approximately 100kg less than its Ferrari rival, an advantage that increased by a further 30kg when each was fuelled ready for a race. At a cornering force of 0.75g the Ferrari would subject its tyres to around 570kg of side load. The Cooper's tyres would not be subjected to a similar force until it was cornering at 0.9g. The compound effect of all this was a breed of car that was less substantial but significantly faster.

A new generation of constructors were building these minimalist machines. Young and ambitious, they were unfettered by convention. Graduates of a post-war British movement of racing, their low-cost, make-do ingenuity overthrew decades of formal training. British racing, which had always lagged behind continental Europe on account of road racing being prohibited by law, was now freshly liberated by scores of disused wartime airfields. A new wave of driving and engineering talent came to the fore, and the financially straitened circumstances of the country only seemed to intensify inventiveness. So it was that a Cooper, using a bought-in engine, a modified road-car gearbox and sundry bits of Citroëns and Triumph Heralds in its workings, overcame the thoroughbreds. And lined right up behind Cooper were a host of imitators, some of them even more talented.

The opening salvo of the 1966 Monaco Grand Prix and Jim Clark's Lotus 33 is right at the back of the pack. He had qualified on pole position for the first race of the new 3-litre formula – even though his car only had a 2-litre Coventry Climax V8 fitted – but he found himself stuck in first gear at the start and the other cars streamed past. Eventually it freed and he began scything through the field. He got as high as third place before his suspension failed. Jackie Stewart scored BRM's fourth consecutive Monaco win.

FAR LEFT: Phil Hill was quicker than 1961 title rival and team-mate Wolfgang von Trips, as evinced by his tally of five pole positions to the German's one. But he struggled to find the same desire in the races. At Zandvoort, von Trips beat him to the victory by just nine-tenths of a second.

LEFT: Team-mates Roy Salvadori (left) and John Surtees relax as their Lola Mk4s are prepared for the 1962 Monaco Grand Prix. On the truck in the background Rob Walker Racing is still billed as being in partnership with Stirling Moss, though Moss was by this time barely out of his coma after his career-ending shunt at Goodwood earlier in the season.

This new breed made aggressively advanced racing cars from limited resources without even subjecting themselves to the grace of an F1 apprenticeship. And given that minimalism was an inherent part of the movement's creed, its cars were frail. Lighter, faster and frailer, the cars may have lacked the visual danger of their 1950s counterparts, but they were in reality at least as lethal. In keeping with the moving times of the outside world, the drivers were no longer matadors but ground-level test pilots.

A concerned governing body tried to slow them down by decreeing a maximum engine size of just 1.5 litres for 1961, but still the lap times tumbled. Even Enzo Ferrari – who had once said he would never build a mid-engined car because the horse should always pull the cart, not push it – was forced to eat his words and produced a Cooper-copy for '61. Ironically, the change in engine regulations put his team in good stead as it produced its own motors, while the Brits had their momentum briefly checked by the lack of a decently powerful bought-in unit of the requisite capacity. So the world championship would be fought over by Ferrari's two leading drivers, Phil Hill and Wolfgang von Trips.

Hill won the title, becoming the first American to do so. But his account of the year gives insight into the fear that could surround even a top driver during this era – if, that is, he questioned himself too much about what he was doing.

For Hill, the good car had come perhaps a season or so too late.

Not that he wasn't still quick – he set five pole positions that year – but his desire had been hurt by the horrendous toll of human life he'd witnessed during his few years in the sport. "More and more guys were getting killed around me," he says today. "At first you rationalise to yourself why it was him and not you, the things that he did that you wouldn't do. But then another would be killed and that didn't apply to him. You had to keep rewriting the script in your head as to why it wasn't you. But eventually – and this point had come to me around 1961 – you realise it's nothing more than plain dumb luck. You start to identify more and more with the guys who've died until, eventually, it's a real struggle to believe it was their inadequacies that were doing them in rather than fate."

Von Trips didn't seem to have reached this stage. "He worried me," admits Hill. "He was extremely fair and very sporting. There was not a trace of the arrogance that you might have expected from someone of his aristocratic upbringing. But he did have what I saw as a difficulty in drawing the line on the track. Over his career he was involved in too many incidents at a time when that was really bad news. There wasn't anything cold or calculated about it; he believed intensely in the honour of the sport and relished the man-to-man challenge. But he worried me because his feel for the limit seemed kinda fuzzy at times.

"In 1961, with a good car at last, he seemed so freaked out about the possibility of becoming world champion that he was

OPPOSITE: The career of the great Moss ended when his Lotus 18/21 slammed into this earth bank during Goodwood's Easter Monday Meeting of 1962. The accident happened in the Glover Trophy, a non-championship race. Moss had lost a lap because of a pit stop to rectify a gearbox problem but, Moss being Moss, he was charging through the field – and was about to unlap himself from the BRM of race leader, and eventual winner, Graham Hill – when he ran wide onto the grass at the very fast Fordwater bend. He impacted at over 100mph.

FAR LEFT: Denny Hulme (in car) came up through the ranks with the Brabham team, scoring Formula Junior, Formula Two and Tasman Series wins for it before Jack (left) gave him his F1 chance in 1965. In the early days Denny also drove the team's truck!

LEFT: Bruce McLaren sits disappointed at the 1965 Dutch Grand Prix having retired his Cooper with gearbox failure. He was by this time already making plans to set up McLaren Racing to build his own F1 cars.

trying extra hard. This was at a time when I'd kinda lost my spirit for racing. He was just way more turned on by it all than I was then, and that was helping him have a real strong season."

At the Italian Grand Prix, the penultimate race of the season, von Trips was killed, along with several spectators, when he interlocked wheels with the Lotus of Jim Clark and was catapulted into the fencing. Hill won the race and the title. He'd seen von Trips's wreck but not the accident, which had happened behind him, and so was unsure about the outcome: "I got out of the car and asked [engineer] Carlo Chiti, 'How's Trips?' I knew from his response – 'Oh, they need you up on the podium now. You must go up on the podium' – what the truth was." What should have been his moment of triumph was one of utter desolation.

For 1962 the British teams got power parity with Ferrari thanks to new V8 engines from Coventry Climax and BRM, and their chassis superiority put them back on top. But it was all too late for Tony Brooks; dejected after a poor year with BRM, he'd retired.

"The change to mid-engined cars took a lot away from the driver," Brooks contends. "They were much easier to drive: very manoeuvrable, easy to get the power down, and the improved roadholding completely changed the power-to-grip ratio so you no longer had the excess of power that allowed you to drift the car on the throttle, especially so after they limited the engines to 1.5 litres. Some guys who you had simply discounted in front-engined cars

suddenly became serious competitors in the mid-engined cars. There was so much less skill required."

Yet Moss continued to display his genius – and his differing technique to Brooks is the likely explanation for their contrasting fortunes. In the front-engined day, when power overwhelmed grip, the key to being quick – the drift – came predominantly from apex to exit, the part of the corner where the driver was controlling the power. But when grip overwhelms power, the critical part of the turn moves back: entry to apex becomes critical. The ability to keep up momentum in this unstable, power-off phase of the corner was what now differentiated the great from the good. Moss had always been able to take more speed into a corner than anyone else, and this now played to his advantage more than ever before. It helped that he was a child of the mid-engine generation, having cut his racing teeth in 500cc Formula Three, the cheap, bike-engined British series responsible for Cooper and the subsequent revolution in F1.

For 1960 his entrant Rob Walker switched Moss from a Cooper to a Lotus, a faster, more advanced car. Its designer, Colin Chapman, took the search of speed to the limit, even by the standards of F1. He improved upon the basic Cooper blueprint by making a chassis with a far more scientific arrangement of metal tubes to give a stiffer construction that transferred cornering loads to the tyres far more effectively. His suspension geometry dramatically reduced weight transfer under cornering load, giving

OPPOSITE: Rescuers extract an unconscious Stirling Moss from a space frame that has collapsed around him. His injuries were grievous – and numerous: badly bruised brain, crushed cheekbone, displaced eye socket, broken left arm, broken left knee, broken left ankle, broken nose and torn muscles. He was in a coma for several weeks. Early in 1963 Moss returned to Goodwood to test a Lotus sports car in order to determine whether he still had the skills to return to F1. Although he set competitive times, he felt his judgement was impaired. Reluctantly, he decided to retire. With the hindsight of many years he considers that both the test and the decision were premature.

FAR LEFT: Reigning world champion Graham Hill began his defence in 1969 with a second place for Team Lotus in South Africa. He ended the season with a violent accident in America that broke his legs. Although he recovered to drive a Lotus the following year, it would be a privateer machine run by Rob Walker. On the pit counter behind Hill and Colin Chapman is Graham's lap-charting wife, Bette.

LEFT: The strength and weakness of the Ferrari 156 are shown here. The strength was its V6 engine, which provided the car with a 30bhp advantage over its British rivals in 1961. The weakness was its crude chassis. When the more advanced British cars got power parity the following year, the Ferrari was rendered an also-ran.

the heavier-loaded outer tyres an easier time and thereby allowing more cornering grip.

But these higher limits made the Lotus a more demanding car than the Cooper. "You couldn't take such liberties with the Lotus," says Moss. "It was quicker, but if you were good enough to get a Lotus to go quicker than a Cooper at that time, boy, you were good."

It was also a more fragile car. Moss broke his back in practice for the Belgian Grand Prix that year when a wheel fell off due to a hub failure, but he came back in time to win the final race of the year in America. "Afterwards there was a reception," he says. "It was my birthday and they brought in a cake with a little racing car on the top of it. When I cut the cake I cut a wheel off the car and said, 'I dedicate this to Colin'. He wasn't very amused."

In 1961 Moss's privateer Lotus took the fight to the more powerful Ferraris, twice defeating them through sheer virtuosity. But early in '62 his career came to a violent end when his Lotus left the track at Goodwood and slammed into an earth bank. The car folded and Moss's life hung in the balance for several weeks.

Although he eventually made a full recovery, Moss never drove a Grand Prix car in anger again. But always the baton is passed, and the natural heir was a young Scot, Jim Clark, who was driving for the works Lotus team, allying his almost

supernatural skill with Chapman's design genius. It was a formidable partnership and few were in any doubt that all records would succumb to them in time.

"I remember qualifying at Monaco in 1961," says Moss, "when Clark, who was still very new and inexperienced, pretty much equalled my time. He wasn't yet the Jim Clark he subsequently became, but I remember saying to Rob [Walker], 'We're not going to get away with running last year's car for very much longer. I'm going to need a car that's the same as his'. The writing was on the wall. I couldn't afford to give him anything. He was made even more formidable by working so closely with Chapman; Colin could interpret what he was saying and really get the best out of him."

Clark and Lotus went on to dominate most of the remainder of the 1.5-litre formula, in force until the end of 1965. During this time he had a team-mate, Trevor Taylor, who neatly summarises Clark's skill: "I'd follow him into a corner thinking, 'By God, he's going to go off at that speed'. Then he'd just somehow gather it all together, and by the time I got through the corner he was disappearing into the next one. I've no idea how he did it, it was like magic. Even now it makes the hairs on the back of my neck stand up just thinking how good he was."

OPPOSITE: The Lotus team at the 1960 Dutch Grand Prix. Boss and design genius Chapman (left) with his drivers: Innes Ireland, Clark and Alan Stacey. Ireland finished second, Stacey retired from third with a broken gearbox, Clark retired from fifth for the same reason. This was Clark's Grand Prix debut. Two weeks later Stacey – who raced despite an artificial lower right leg – was killed at the Belgian Grand Prix; it is believed that a bird flew into his face and knocked him out. Clark was the first to arrive at the scene of the crash and afterwards seriously considered retiring from the sport. But he couldn't.

Jim Clark shoots into a short-lived lead at the 1963 German Grand Prix; his Lotus's engine is about to misfire, allowing the BRM of Richie Ginther (2) to overtake him. The race, however, will be won by Ferrari's John Surtees (7). Also in shot are the Coopers of Bruce McLaren (5) and Tony Maggs (6), Lorenzo Bandini's semi-works BRM run by Scuderia Centro Sud (15) and Willy Mairesse's Ferrari (8). 'Wild Willy' was returning to the cockpit after a spell in hospital recovering from burns incurred at Le Mans. At the end of the first lap he put himself straight back there, crashing out after getting off-line at the Nürburgring's Flugplatz jump. He broke an arm in an accident that also killed a medical assistant.

LEFT: The Nürburgring wasn't all about bends. This is the long undulating straight that brought its 14-mile lap to a close. John Surtees (Ferrari 156/63) enjoys a comfortable lead over Jim Clark's Lotus 25 on the way to his breakthrough victory in the 1963 German Grand Prix. Surtees – a former multiple world motorcycle champion – would go on to take the F1 title in 1964, but his career in cars was put in the shade by Clark's. Yet there is evidence to suggest that only their choice of machinery separated their relative success. The Nürburgring was considered the ultimate test of a driver and twice Surtees beat Clark here. The high hedges that lined much of the track – until it was 'updated' in the early 1970s – led to the 'Ring's unofficial title: The Green Hell.

RIGHT: Silverstone 1967. Clark demonstrates that the art of the four-wheel drift is far from dead. The Lotus 49 did not fill him with confidence initially, even though it was by far the fastest car of the time. He felt the abrupt power delivery of the Cosworth DFV upset its handling balance: "It's as if the car gets up on its back wheels as you turn into a corner, and then the back end tends to flick out very suddenly." He still won, though – his fifth British Grand Prix victory in six years.

LEFT: The Ferrari team don overcoats for the unfamiliarly chilly surroundings of Aintree, scene of the 1962 British Grand Prix. This was the last time that the Liverpool track hosted the race, having done so on five occasions since 1955. The young man in the horn-rimmed spectacles – and seemingly more at ease with the northerly climes – is future Ferrari design great Mauro Forghieri, already several years into his career with Enzo's squad.

TOP RIGHT: A critical moment in the 1964 title race. Tony Rudd, BRM's chief designer, and Graham Hill discuss a disappointing qualifying session at the German Grand Prix. Hill could do no better than fifth-fastest, 5.4 seconds slower than the pole-winning Ferrari of John Surtees. Hill's car would suffer a misfire in the race and finish a distant second to Surtees. This success was the springboard to the latter's successful late-season charge to the title. Hill would finish runner-up in that 'race' too – just one point shy of his ultimate goal.

BOTTOM RIGHT: Showing remarkably few signs of the severe injuries he'd received at Goodwood just six months before, Stirling Moss chats to Hill in the Monza pits in 1962. The latter would win the Italian Grand Prix for BRM – and eventually take that year's title. At this point Moss was hoping to return to racing once fit.

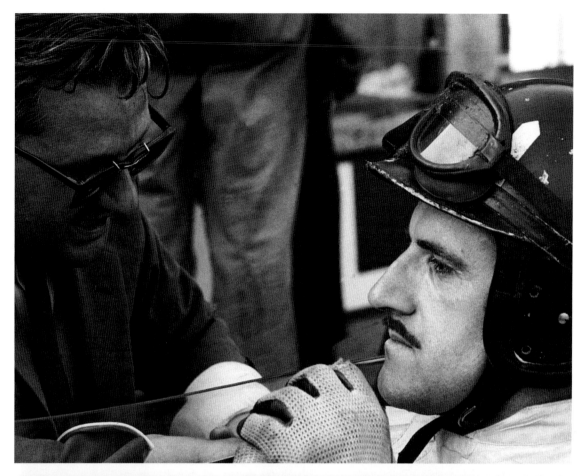

LEFT: **Monza, September 12, 1965.** The Italian Grand Prix gets under way in a haze of rubber smoke. The crowd is beginning to groan as John Surtees, in their beloved red Ferrari, starts very slowly due to a dragging clutch. Meanwhile, Jim Clark (far right) and Jackie Stewart (slightly in the lead) fight out who's going to reach Curva Grande first. Surtees completed the first lap down in 14th place but fought back magnificently in the powerful new Ferrari 1512 to be leading by lap 11. He was unable to pull away, however, for the other cars were able to get a tow from his slipstream – F1 air had yet to be made 'dirty' by wings. The lead see-sawed between Surtees, Clark, Graham Hill and Stewart – until the Ferrari's clutch finally failed on lap 34. Thirty laps later Clark retired his Lotus 33 from the lead with broken fuel injection, leaving the two BRM P261s to battle it out. Stewart pressured Hill into an error at the final corner of the last lap and scored his first Grand Prix victory.

TOP RIGHT: The first lap of the 1960 French Grand Prix, held on public roads near Reims. The cars will bear right; had they gone straight on they would have been following the line of the old circuit, down to a tight right-hander in the village of Gueux, that had been used for this race until 1951. But this was an age when circuits vied to be the world's fastest and so this sweeping bend was added to the track's three long straights. The powerful Ferrari 246 Dinos had been predicted to go well here, and Phil Hill leads his *Scuderia* team-mates Wolfgang von Trips and Willy Mairesse into the first corner. But tucked down among them is the Cooper T53 of Jack Brabham, the eventual winner. Even at this track, F1's new wave could not be turned back: Coopers finished 1-2-3-4.

BOTTOM RIGHT: Jack Brabham acknowledges victory in the 1960 French Grand Prix from 'Toto' Roche, the flamboyant official who ran the event whenever its venue was Reims. Known for his highly unpredictable technique in starting the race, Roche would often drop the flag whilst still standing on the grid and have cars swerving around him as he ran for cover. After being pushed initially by the Ferrari of Phil Hill until it retired, Brabham won in commanding fashion – almost 50s ahead of the older model Cooper of Olivier Gendebien. On a track that should have suited the powerful but old fashioned front-engined Ferraris, the little Coopers were just as fast down the straights, gaining through smaller frontal area what they lost with their power disadvantage. Brabham was reaching 180mph at the fastest point of the track.

LEFT: Jim Clark, delayed at the start of the 1962 Monaco Grand Prix by a fouled spark plug, charges back through the field. Constantly resetting and breaking the lap record, he was closing in on Graham Hill for the lead when his Lotus 25's clutch failed. Monaco was a race Clark was destined never to win despite several brilliant performances. Hill, in contrast, won it five times. On this occasion, however, it would slip through his fingers too, his BRM's engine breaking seven laps from the finish, handing the win to Bruce McLaren's Cooper.

TOP RIGHT: Colin Chapman and Clark, world champions together in 1963 and '65, were forever powering the other onto yet greater heights. Chapman was devastated by Clark's death and vowed never again to become as close to one of his drivers. Here they celebrate their fifth win of the 1963 season, the Italian Grand Prix. There were still two more to come that year: America and Mexico.

BOTTOM RIGHT: A 1964 British Grand Prix lap of honour for Clark, Chapman and some of Lotus's hardworking troops – including chief mechanic Jim Endruweit. "Lotus hadn't been a terribly happy outfit before it started winning," he recalls. "But when we started winning it was a total transformation. Plus we had, in my opinion, the number one driver of all time in Jim. The guys would do anything for him. Everybody knew that if they did their bit right, Jim would do his – and we'd win."

Jo Bonnier's BRM P48 led the early laps of the 1960 Monaco Grand Prix but was eventually passed by Stirling Moss, here lying third behind Jack Brabham's Cooper T53. Moss would go on to score Lotus's first Grand Prix victory, but not Team Lotus's – his 18 model was run privately by Rob Walker.

Phil Hill's Ferrari 246 Dino rounds the Station Hairpin in the 1960 Monaco Grand Prix. Note the flexion of the right-front tyre, something that Lotus's Colin Chapman was working flat-out to eradicate, but which Ferrari was not yet concerned about.

Richie Ginther's Ferrari 156 takes the lead at the start of the 1961 Monaco Grand Prix. The American would put in the drive of his life, setting a startling fastest lap in the process. Unfortunately for him, Moss also delivered what he personally considers his greatest-ever drive to win – and equal Ginther's fastest lap – in a year-old Lotus. Going round the outside of Moss here, though, is Jim Clark in the new Lotus 21 (28). The young Scot had qualified on the front row but would have his race spoiled by a persistent misfire. Even so, it was at this time that Moss says he first recognised the threat Clark was going to represent.

Although Monaco's general backdrop looks familiar, this section of track is now much changed; the old Gasworks Hairpin was swamped by new buildings in the early 1970s.

From Black-and-White to Colour

Jim Clark scored his 25th Grand Prix victory on New Year's Day 1968 in South Africa, thereby surpassing the total of the previous record-holder Juan Manuel Fangio. It was the brilliant Scot's final appearance in the world championship. Four months later he was dead, the world's greatest driver snatched away at 32, killed in an unimportant F2 race at Hockenheim, Germany.

The second round of the championship wasn't until May, in Spain. There Graham Hill put some spirit back into the devastated Lotus team by winning. As Clark had in South Africa, he drove a Lotus 49 – only now it looked very different. Clark's car had been finished in the team's familiar scheme of green – Britain's official racing colour – with a central yellow stripe; Hill's was decorated like a cigarette packet, in Gold Leaf's red-and-gold brand livery. Commercial sponsorship had arrived in F1 and with it came an explosion of colour. As pop went psychedelic arm in arm with the drug culture, F1 'flowered' thanks to the most powerful drug of all: money.

The timing was spookily apt. Clark, an introvert from farming stock, would have been a square in a necessarily more rounded role. But fellow Scot Jackie Stewart could not have been better suited to the sport's brash new world. A genius driver, he was also full-on, garrulous, articulate and commercially astute: the figurehead for the commercial electrification of the sport.

Stewart had, though, just lost his mentor and close friend: "I first heard about Jimmy's accident when I was doing a track safety inspection at Jarama. They didn't give it to me full blast first time around. Then they came back and said it was a very serious accident and that it didn't look good. But they still didn't tell me until much later that he'd died. I was devastated. He was Mr Infallible, Mr Clean.

"Later, after the shock, I guess there was some conflict in me about who was going to take over his mantle. But life goes on. I was bright-eyed and bushy-tailed. Why shouldn't it be me? On the one hand I felt his loss deeply – we used to travel together, eat together – on the other, professionally, I came of age that year."

Stewart was ready to make his own mark. Soon came the long hair, fashionable shades and threads. He was a high-speed icon, a brand in his own right: 'Jackie Stewart, master of going faster'. He transcended the sport yet brought it with him, imposing its presence, increasing its brand awareness. There he is with The Beatles, here he talks to Elizabeth Taylor at a film premiere, now he's all charm and humour on a TV chat show.

And then he climbs into his Elf-sponsored F1 Matra – a car made by a missile manufacturer, how moon shot is that? – at a foggy, rainy Nürburgring. The electric guitar soundtrack of his life fades to a silence broken only by clanking spanners. The layers of gloss are peeled back as he sits alone, earplugs and helmet drowning out the extraneous. Then the Cosworth DFV stabs him in the back and suddenly the gladiatorial basics of his sport are brought home. Forcibly. Where are his showbiz friends now? At parties, ingesting substances? This is real.

Out he goes, 160mph between the trees in near-zero visibility. And he wins. By over four minutes. He's escaped with his life yet again. The party continues, brand enhanced, dollars racking up.

Chris Amon's Ferrari 312/69 rounds Gasworks hairpin in glorious technicolour, Monaco 1969. The car's high wing tells you this is Thursday practice as the governing body banned wings before the following session on Saturday. After a brilliant but unlucky 1968 season, Amon was left sorely disappointed with the car provided by Ferrari for '69. "It was still powered by what was really just a converted sports car engine. It made a great noise but it was big and heavy and although they claimed 435 horsepower, I know for a fact it was down on power to the '68 engine and that only had around 400. At Monaco I got it onto the front row and I was running second in the race to Jackie [Stewart], both of us ahead of Graham [Hill], who eventually won. But to get it to perform like that round there you had to be really brutal with it because the engine was so peaky and eventually it broke its transmission."

Stewart's driving talent was always his major attribute, but his shrewdness in recognising what he needed to get the best from himself was never far behind. In this, his partnership with Ken Tyrrell – the man who discovered him and later established the F1 team that would take both of them to glory – was critical. In its way their connection was every bit as effective as that between Jim Clark and Colin Chapman. Only this time it was the driver who brought Ford Motor Company to the table, not the team boss. Stewart's greatest achievement was being the first to recognise that talent alone would no longer shape the F1 history books.

Just ask John Surtees. The former motorcycling world champion, who repeated the achievement in cars in 1964, was a giant of a driver blessed with the skills required to take on Clark or Stewart on equal terms. But he was rarely on equal terms – even though he'd had a head start; he was in situ at Lotus in 1960 when Clark was recruited as his stand-in. It was only when Surtees walked from the team that Clark gained full-time membership. And this was just the first of several questionable career moves.

"I still possess the Lotus contract giving me the option of who I wanted as team-mate for 1961 – Jimmy or Innes Ireland," says Surtees. "I chose Jimmy and that brought about my break-up with the team. Innes got very irate. There was one hell of a fuss that created a lot of ill feeling. I was being perceived as this new boy in the game and so I walked away from it. I don't necessarily think it was a bad move in hindsight; if I hadn't done it, I doubt whether I'd be here to tell the story.

"We'd gone from a period where we had somewhat antiquated but well-engineered designs to a new era of more advanced design but poorer engineering. I think the cars I drove subsequently – the Ferraris, Hondas and Coopers – were perhaps better-engineered, safer cars than the Lotuses, but not as fast."

Surtees secured his championship with Ferrari and looked set to take another for the team in 1966. But as a strong-willed man in a volatile team, he fell foul of the politics: "In an Italian team – and I found this in motorcycles as well as cars – you need to be sure of yourself and behave as if you're sure of yourself, and then prove it by performance. Otherwise you're finished. That's what I did, but in doing so I fell foul of certain people." After a row with team manager Eugenio Dragoni, Surtees left in high dudgeon. "There was a title there for the taking in 1966 when I left, and perhaps another in '67, maybe even a third in '68. Many years later Mr Ferrari said to me, 'We must remember the good times and not the mistakes'. I said I couldn't agree more. The split wasn't good for either of us. We both went into a barren patch."

Surtees had now turned his back on Lotus *and* Ferrari, the pre-eminent teams of the era, and a driver that had gone wheel to wheel with Clark in his formative car years never really found his way back despite soldiering on into the early 1970s.

"In many ways – and I don't say this unkindly – the man whose career gained the most from Jimmy's death was Jackie Stewart," says Surtees. "Jackie learned a lot from the mistakes that had occurred in Jimmy's business life. And what's more, had Jimmy lived he would've remained Ford's number one man and there wouldn't have been a mantle for Jackie to pick up."

FAR LEFT: Colin Chapman and Jochen Rindt read what's been written about them. Although not employed at Lotus until almost a year after Jim Clark was killed, Rindt's phenomenal speed ensured he was the Scot's true replacement at the team. But the respective relationships of each driver with Chapman could hardly have been more different. Rindt and Chapman, both aggressive and combative, endured many arguments, often over Rindt's misgivings about the safety of the cars. He had joined the team knowing that it would probably provide him with the fastest car, but he was also well aware that it was a career move that compromised his chances of survival. He was killed in 1970, in a Monza practice crash that many believe was caused by a mechanical failure.

LEFT: Facilities during the 1960s were still rudimentary. Here's the timing HQ and leader board for the 1964 Austrian Grand Prix, held on a makeshift circuit at a military airfield. Ferrari's Lorenzo Bandini (8) is just 10 laps away from scoring his only Grand Prix win.

ABOVE: The Ferrari 312 of Jonathan Williams leads Jean-Pierre Beltoise's F2 Matra MS7 in the 1967 Mexican Grand Prix. This was the only Grand Prix Williams – an Englishman based in Italy – ever contested. He finished eighth, two laps behind the winning Lotus 49 of Clark. Beltoise, in his third Grand Prix, all of them to date at the wheel of a Formula Two car, finished seventh.

FAR LEFT: **Loose spanners, paper cups, a spare wheel lying in the grass, a deck chair for a perch: the pit lane ambience of the 1960s could hardly be more different from the high-gloss F1 world of today. The bond between Jim Clark and Colin Chapman was still very strong by 1967 – this photo was taken at that year's Canadian Grand Prix at Mosport – but Clark's friend Jackie Stewart believes Jim was becoming more independent, more critical, and that "Colin was going to start having problems with him". Clark set pole and fastest lap at this race, but retired because of ignition problems.**

LEFT: **Mike Parkes enjoys a relaxing cup of tea shortly after putting his Ferrari 312 on pole position for the 1966 Italian Grand Prix. The Englishman was very much a favourite of Enzo Ferrari's – but there was a major point of conflict in their relationship: Ferrari valued his engineering skill, but Parkes wanted to race at the highest level. When John Surtees left the team in the middle of 1966 Enzo relented and gave Parkes his head. He even had the team build a long-chassis car to accommodate Mike's lanky frame. He showed well, scoring two second places, including here at Monza, but eight months after this photograph was taken Parkes crashed in the 1967 Belgian Grand Prix and received the severe leg injuries that ended his F1 career.**

RIGHT: **The beautiful 'Sharknose' Ferrari 156s attract attention at Spa in the lead-up to the 1961 Belgian Grand Prix. They would take the first four places, winner Phil Hill (4) supported by Wolfgang von Trips (2), Richie Ginther (6) and local hero Olivier Gendebien, whose car (not seen here) was painted in the yellow of the Ecurie Nationale Belge team.**

FAR LEFT: Jackie Stewart's Matra MS80 leads Jack Brabham's Brabham BT26A around the stunning Montjuich Park circuit in the 1969 Spanish Grand Prix. Although beautiful, this Barcelona track ultimately wasn't safe enough for the coming era. Stewart won on this occasion – by two clear laps.

LEFT: Jim Clark enjoys the victory spoils in Mexico, 1967. He didn't know it, but his clock was already counting down. The tradition of presenting a Grand Prix winner with a laurel wreath was halted when sponsors began complaining that they were covering up their logos during this ideal photo opportunity.

This image shouldn't really be spread over two pages. Its quality is too grainy to stand up to such amplification. But its composition is so beautiful, the atmosphere of early 1960s Monte Carlo so perfectly captured, that it had to stay this way.

Ferrari's Phil Hill has just swapped the darkness of Monaco's tunnel for the blinding sunlight of its harbour. His foot is hard down, his bruised gear-change hand looks like a slab of meat. After 100 punishing laps the flag falls and he finds himself in third place. The year is 1960.

How Do I Get Out of this Alive?

Jackie Stewart, icon, did something useful with his profile. His every utterance backed up by the steely courage and flawless perfection of his on-track performances, he took on The Establishment. With his friends being slain around him, he saw no reason why the sport had to be as downright lethal as it was. So he began a crusade, one that would last several years but which would finally rid the sport of some of its barbaric excesses.

For him, it had been triggered by the 1966 Belgian Grand Prix. Held on closed public roads through the Ardennes, pressure changes caused by variations in altitude and thick forestation made Spa's weather notoriously schizophrenic. The race began in the dry. But even as the cars sped away, a storm was breaking out on the far side of the track, i.e. in an adjacent valley. The pack entered the village of Malmédy at 130mph – and hit a wall of water. Cars were spinning everywhere, between the houses, stone walls, telegraph poles and barbed wire fences. Stewart glanced off a wall and plunged into a ditch, the impact trapping him in the cockpit by the steering wheel – and rupturing the fuel tanks.

Not only could Stewart smell the fuel, he could feel it. It had saturated him. No marshals were there to free him and he waited in horror, waited for the hot exhausts to ignite the gallons of fuel that were leaching around him. Mercifully, they didn't, and two drivers – Graham Hill and Bob Bondurant – whose cars had also crashed out, came to his rescue. But they needed to remove the BRM's steering wheel and no one had a spanner. A marshal was found and he eventually sourced one from a spectator's car. Twenty minutes after the accident Stewart was extricated, a shoulder broken, his kidneys bruised.

There was no medical back-up and Hill had to phone for help. Stewart's fuel-saturated overalls were burning his skin and had to be removed as he was laid out in a farm building. Forty minutes after the accident a circuit ambulance arrived. It was full of nurses who promptly tried to re-cover Stewart's nether regions with his overalls to save their embarrassment. There seemed to be no embarrassment, however, about the filthy state of the track's medical centre, its floor covered in cigarette butts, or the fact that the ambulance driver taking Stewart to the local hospital got lost on the way there.

To his amazement, Graham Hill climbs out unscathed after a snapped wing stalk has sent his Lotus airborne and thence into the barriers during the 1969 Spanish Grand Prix. Six years later, at the very same place, Hill's race-leading car – driven by Rolf Stommelen – suffered a near-identical accident, but this time three race officials and a photographer were killed as the wreckage vaulted the barrier. The spooky coincidences didn't stop there. Before the 1975 race there had been a row between the teams and the race organisers about the inadequate way the barriers had been secured. The end result was that team personnel themselves went out tightening bolts. Stommelen hit the very section of barrier on which the Hill mechanics had worked. They had even written a jokey note on it: 'Rolf, please stay off!' Stommelen suffered a broken leg and wrist in an accident caused by the collapse of a rear wing stay.

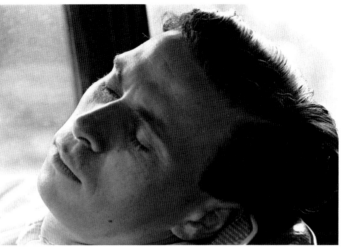

FAR LEFT: **Jack Brabham in conference with his designer Ron Tauranac. This pair had worked together on the dirt tracks in Australia, and when Brabham left Cooper to set up on his own he had no hesitation in bringing Tauranac over to England. When Brabham sold up at the end of 1970, Tauranac took over the business. But he didn't enjoy it without his former partner and sold it in turn to Bernie Ecclestone.**

LEFT: **Jim Clark takes a nap before the 1963 German Grand Prix. His Lotus would finish second to the Ferrari of John Surtees after being compromised by a faulty spark plug. This was the only time Clark was beaten all year. In every other race he either won or retired.**

As an illustration of how low a priority was given to racing drivers' lives it was stark, verging on criminal. For the next couple of years Stewart concentrated on maximising his own chances of survival by adopting the newfangled fireproof racewear, with his blood group embroidered into it – and by taping a spanner to his steering wheel!

But Stewart the celebrity, the regular Grand Prix winner, close runner-up in the 1968 world championship, '69 world champion – that Stewart – was able to do something more. As leader of a drivers association, the GPDA, he became militant, demanding changes be made to circuits before allowing his members to race there. He insisted trackside trees were felled, barbed wire fences removed and protective barriers erected at key danger spots. Circuit medical centres had to be upgraded. Helicopters had to be on standby to ferry injured drivers to hospital. Some tracks, notably Spa, were deemed intrinsically too dangerous and lost their place on the championship calendar.

Common sense, all of it. Yet Stewart's campaign met with resistance, even indignation. Brands Hatch tried to charge him the expense it incurred in felling its trees. Certain drivers were staunch supporters, notably Stewart's close friend and rival Jochen Rindt, whose style in a car was aggressive and uncompromising; it was almost as if Rindt, once out of the car, recognised that he needed to be protected from his addicted, competitive self. Others like Jacky Ickx, apparently in love with the fatalistic image they had of their profession, turned their backs on Stewart. This may have made them seem more heroic, but what is so heroic about deriding the efforts of others while at the same time benefiting from them? Today, a more mature Ickx reflects that he and many others owe Stewart a huge debt of gratitude. And their lives.

Grand Prix racing remained a risky occupation, but at least its blatantly unnecessary risks had been removed. The sport lost something in the process. But it probably had to in the long term, at least if it wanted the new-found money to keep on rolling in. Money made the cars go faster, so for the speed junkies there was really no question of priorities to be answered. Stewart may have started out by taking on The Establishment, but eventually its aims and his meshed together rather well.

OPPOSITE: **An identical failure to that of Hill's saw a near-identical crash 11 laps later for Jochen Rindt. His Lotus cannoned off Hill's abandoned wreck and he was lucky to escape with a broken nose. Hill had been running back to the pits in order to warn the team about what had happened to him – but Rindt crashed before he got there.**

TOP LEFT: Phil Hill set pole position and fastest lap at the 1961 German Grand Prix – but again Stirling Moss spoiled Ferrari's day. The inspired British star made light of the changeable conditions in his outdated Lotus to score his second memorable win of the year. A soft-compound Dunlop rain tyre helped him, as did a shower late in the race – without it the Ferraris might have caught him. Hill eventually finished third.

BOTTOM LEFT: New world champion Jack Brabham is giving it his all as he keeps the pressure on the race-leading Cooper-Maserati of John Surtees at the 1966 Mexican Grand Prix. The embedded half-tyres defining the track's edge could be lethally dangerous and were banned a couple of years later.

RIGHT: Tin-kering F1 mechanics. A Coca-Cola can is rigged up as a temporary catch-tank for oil that might overflow from the Honda V12 engine once it is up to running temperature.

It should have been 31-year-old Lorenzo Bandini's breakthrough season, 1967. He'd shown promise in the previous three years but had always been under the shadow of Ferrari team leader John Surtees. But now he was Enzo's senior driver and Monaco represented his first opportunity of the season to score well. Team-mate Chris Amon drove to the track with him from Italy. "It was incredible how badly organised he was," he says. "People used to say that about me, but he topped even that. On the way he had so many things to do, stopping off here, seeing someone there, that it took forever. We didn't arrive in Monte Carlo until about 3am of the morning of first practice." Nonetheless, Bandini qualified on the front row and thrust his red Ferrari into the lead at the drop of the flag. He was later passed by Denny's Hulme's Brabham BT20, which was easier to handle than the heavier Ferrari 312 on a track made slippery by an oil spillage. But as the circuit regained its grip so Bandini came back into the picture, cutting Hulme's lead down from 19 seconds to seven before Hulme stabilised and then extended the gap once more. In the race's late stages Bandini's lines appeared to be getting erratic. "It was a scorching-hot day and a very long race," recalls Amon. "I know I was totally dehydrated and I suspect that's what happened to him." Dehydration, possibly exacerbated by a lack of sleep, a slight loss of concentration, and the tragedy unfolded. Bandini – probably already unconscious from the initial impact – was trapped inside the upturned burning car, firefighters hopelessly inadequately equipped, the flames fanned by a hovering helicopter getting film footage of the incident. He survived for three days before succumbing to his injuries.

The final tragedy was that his traumatised wife, Margherita, suffered a miscarriage.

LEFT: Fury, arrogance and impatience were all part of what made Jochen Rindt the driver he was. Just look at his face, his stance, the chaotic mess of belongings behind him: a human whirlwind. He had his safe side, though. That white crash helmet is the new full-face he has just switched to after years of wrapping a piece of cloth around his mouth, to keep the road dirt out, before pulling on his open-face.

RIGHT: The long hair, shades and cap were very much part of Jackie Stewart's 'branding'.

Pedro Rodriguez locks his brakes as he runs ahead of Lotus team-mate Jim Clark in the 1966 Mexican Grand Prix. Clark, in the BRM H16-powered 43 model, was suffering engine problems and had been passed by Rodriguez, who, to the delight of his countrymen in the crowd, ran as high as third in his 2.1-litre 33 before retiring with a broken final drive late in the race. Rodriguez was at this time only an occasional F1 driver, still torn by his addiction on the one hand and on the other by the fact that the sport had killed his younger brother Ricardo at this very track four years earlier. Pedro succumbed to the addiction, became full-time in 1967 – and was killed in 1971.

Jackie Stewart won the 1968 German Grand Prix – by over four minutes. In the midst of his safety campaign he still had the commitment to climb into a car on a circuit as dangerous as the Nürburgring, in conditions as appalling as these – and dominate. Such performances brought an authority to the campaign that none of his rivals could have matched. His team boss Ken Tyrrell had earlier demanded that Stewart try the car out in similarly dangerous conditions during practice. It was the only time the two men had been known to strongly disagree, Tyrrell noting that he felt extremely uncomfortable making the demand but feeling, too, that it was necessary so that Stewart could learn where the hazards were likely to be in the event of the race taking place in such conditions. Stewart knew that Tyrrell had only his best interests at heart. "I always felt that in driving for Ken I was minimising the danger," he says today. "He had a tremendously responsible attitude towards making a safe car. He didn't always have the very fastest cars because sometimes that would have required making them a bit more marginal from the safety point of view. A case in point was his reluctance to have inboard front brakes; he felt that I could compensate for any small performance penalty that arose from making his cars as safe as possible. That was a very untypical philosophy in F1 and it stretched to how he looked after his staff in general. He was a closet socialist: he would insist that every one of his employees had a pension, for example. That was unheard of in F1; other teams' mechanics might even find themselves laid-off during the off-season."

Stewart always makes much of how 'mind management' was crucial to his devastating performances. Having such confidence in the relative safety of Tyrrell's cars was surely an essential part of compartmentalising the demands he faced and was, therefore, key to races such as this, deemed by many to be his greatest-ever drive.

Something in the Air

Stewart the icon, with his safety crusade, showbiz friends, fashionable clothes and peerless driving was making all the news and the cars had rather faded into the background. But something else was in the air; little eddies of thought, small disturbances deviating from the conventional. They had been gathering for years in the minds of those other speed junkies – the engineers. These streams of consciousness were finally about to converge to bring F1 its most spectacular performance leap since the advent of the mid-engine layout.

The principle involved turning an aircraft wing-shape upside down. When air passes further over a lower surface than an upper one it creates a downwards pressure as the air passing over the rounded underside is forced to accelerate; like a fluid, when air speeds up it loses pressure. With the slower air on the upper surface of the wing having a higher pressure than the faster air on the underside, the wing forces down upon the car through the medium of the tyres. This is downforce.

Tyres oppose whatever force is made upon them and this opposing force is defined as grip. A heavier car induces more grip from its tyres – yet has a lower cornering limit. This apparent paradox is explained by the centrifugal force the extra weight imposes overcoming the increase in grip. So a lighter car needs less tyre grip to attain the same cornering force. Downforce induces extra grip from the tyres by loading them harder, without the centrifugal forces of extra weight. In effect, it cons the tyres into behaving as if they were supporting a greater weight than they are, and roadholding increases accordingly. We know this now. But it took forever for the idea to break through.

In 1928 Opel made its second experimental rocket-powered car, RAK 2. It featured an inverted wing to combat aerodynamic lift at high speeds. In the 1950s a Swiss engineer, Michael May, who was also an amateur racing driver, took up the theme. He mounted such a device over the cockpit of his Porsche Spyder and at a sports car race at the Nürburgring in 1956 outqualified the works Porsches. This led to a protest that led to a ban: his wing impeded the vision of following competitors, apparently. Thus discouraged, May didn't persevere with the idea.

In 1961 Ferrari driver Richie Ginther – a former mechanic in the United States Air Force – came up with an aircraft-inspired flip-up that run along the back of his Ferrari 246 sports-racer; it greatly improved the car's high-speed stability. In 1966 noted Texan driver/engineer Jim Hall incorporated a high wing into the design of his Chaparral 2E sports car. Chaparral was an undercover racing

With their outrageous high wings grinding their tyres into the track, the Lotus 49Bs of Graham Hill and Jo Siffert and the Matra MS10 of Jackie Stewart fight for the lead of the 1968 Mexican Grand Prix. The outcome of this battle in the season finale would determine who between Hill and Stewart would become world champion. Hill won the race and, for the second time in his career, the title.

satellite of General Motors and the initiative came from Chevrolet's research and development engineers.

The concept had been stuttering around for decades, its significance unrecognised, but now momentum began to build; the space dust that preludes the explosive creation of a new star began to heat up. At the time the bewinged Chaparral was first hitting the tracks in America, over in F1, McLaren's chief designer Robin Herd thought he might try the idea out at a test session. Remarkably, despite very encouraging results, he forgot about it!

"It was during a test at Zandvoort with Bruce McLaren," says Herd. "We sent Bruce out with the car as normal, brought him in, fitted the wings and sent him out again. He instantly went two seconds per lap quicker. We couldn't believe it. He came in and said, 'Oh, the car felt better before. That can't be right'. So we repeated the test – and it happened again. We didn't want anyone else to twig, so we took the wings off, quietly put them in the back of the truck and continued with our normal testing. We decided we would look into it further, in private, when we had the time. But an F1 team in those days was so madly understaffed that we never got round to looking at it properly. There were so many other fires to fight."

In practice for the 1967 Belgian Grand Prix at the super-fast Spa track, aerodynamic lift was causing the front end of the Lotus 49s of Jim Clark and Graham Hill to run out of grip at high speed. In earlier times this might have been simply accepted or some mechanical adjustments made. But this time a small bib extension of aluminium, jutting out from beneath the nose, was tried. Another little click on the development ratchet had just unknowingly been made. The bib made the front end of the car too effective for the rear and induced excessive oversteer, so the drivers discarded it. But it meant something, was a little detail for the engineers to file away while their minds wrestled with its greater significance.

In November 1967 Clark took time out from F1 to race an American Champcar, a Vollstedt, that featured small inverted wings; he was impressed with its grip and stability. Clark got to talking with one of his Lotus mechanics about this during a race series, the Tasman, held in New Zealand and Australia while Europe was in the grip of winter. The mechanic fashioned a small rear wing from a helicopter rotor and rigged it to Clark's car. When Colin Chapman found out he was furious and ordered that the device be removed. This was done – but not before a Ferrari engineer had taken photographs of it. More germination.

FAR LEFT: The locals enjoy their refreshments on a sunny day at Reims as Dan Gurney's Eagle T1G passes by during the 1966 French Grand Prix. In establishing his Anglo American Racers team – and its Eagle marque – Gurney was following in the footsteps of driver-turned-constructor Jack Brabham, for whom he had driven in the previous three seasons. Ironically, it was a decision that probably cost Gurney a world championship. Brabham had been planning to retire from driving for 1966 and have Gurney as his lead driver; and that year's Brabham proved to be the class of the field. But it was Brabham piloting it to championship glory, not Gurney. Dan instead found himself struggling in an underpowered car. On this particular occasion it was lapped three times by the race winner: Jack Brabham.

Chapman was already thinking along aerodynamic lines for the design of his next Indianapolis challenger, the Lotus 56. It featured an upswept profile with a flat expanse of upper bodywork at the rear designed to give a measure of downforce. When he then updated his F1 car, the Lotus 49, he applied a similar principle to its new bodywork. In addition, to balance out the downforce produced at the rear, he incorporated adjustable-angle front 'winglets'. This car first appeared at the 1968 Monaco Grand Prix.

A fortnight later, at the Belgian Grand Prix, two rival teams – Brabham and Ferrari – appeared with full inverted wings at the rear of their cars; Chris Amon's Ferrari took pole position by the huge margin of 3.7 seconds. There was something in the air – grip, masses of it. Downforce had finally arrived in F1. The genie was out of the bottle.

Brabham's designer Ron Tauranac remembers its development: "We knew we were getting lift with the cars at speed. We knew that was costing us time in the fast corners. So we just thought about ways of getting some downforce on the car. We made a new engine cover and incorporated the wing into that, and took it to Spa, untried. Spa was our wind tunnel, in effect. Jack [Brabham] said it was just like someone had a hand pressing down on the car, steadying it."

"We had no idea Ferrari were thinking along similar lines. They turned up with theirs at the same race – just by chance, I think."

Maybe. What is sure is that there was a lot of cross-pollination of ideas going on. Ferrari's chief engineer Mauro Forghieri, his memory perhaps triggered by that Tasman photo taken by one of his staff of that experimental Lotus wing, had recalled that Michael May – the engineer with whom he had worked perfecting Ferrari's fuel injection system a few years earlier – had once made a wing for that sports car of his. "Michael was a friend as well as a consultant," says Forghieri. "He told me about the improvement in handling of his winged Porsche. The Chaparral convinced us even more about the idea." It may also be significant that Forghieri was around at Ferrari when Ginther had come up with the trim-tab idea in 1961.

Proving that engineers are every bit as competitive as drivers, Forghieri isn't convinced that Brabham had its wing before it left for Spa: "It only appeared on the second day of practice – after Amon had made a very good time on the first day. I believe they made it overnight after seeing ours."

Chapman had been leapfrogged. Not for long. Two races later his Lotuses appeared with their wings mounted, not to the body

ABOVE LEFT: Graham Hill's high-wing Lotus 49B at Monaco in 1969. The aerodynamic loads of the rear wing were fed directly to the wheel hubs, a very effective way of putting load into the tyres – but a dangerous one. Sudden spike loadings from road bumps could be beyond the load-bearing capability of either the suspension or the wing stalks – another manifestation of the competitive addiction in F1. And so they were banned – between this practice session and the race itself. Despite this, Hill went on to score his fifth – and final – Monaco victory.

FAR LEFT: Suspension-mounted wings as fitted to the 1968 Brabham BT26. Despite safety misgiving, designer Ron Tauranac followed where Lotus had led. This illustrates the agonising dilemma often faced by F1 designers of the time between safety and performance, with the latter invariably winning out.

LEFT: Jim Clark used the same set of Dunlops to win several Grands Prix in the middle of the 1963 season. The very even wear patterns on these rear tyres is probably significant. In 1966 Firestone conducted research into how F1 drivers differed in their use of tyres and found that there was generally a significant wear pattern difference front:rear and left:right for most drivers once the various loads of each circuit were taken into account. With Clark there was only a five per cent difference front:rear and virtually none left:right. No other driver came close to these figures.

like those of Brabham and Ferrari, but to the rear wheel uprights, feeding the loads directly and therefore far more efficiently.

"That was always going to be a more effective place to put them, as it worked directly on the suspension," says Tauranac. "But it was also more dangerous because you couldn't really design a structure strong enough to withstand the forces and those of the road bumps. We followed Chapman only because we had to. We weren't comfortable doing it."

The wings, as well as creating downforce, which was good, also created drag, which was bad. The good more than overcame the bad but, as ever, F1 wanted the best of all worlds and so began devising wings that were retractable on the straights. They also got mounted ever higher, moving them out of the choppy airflow around the car and into more efficient 'cleaner' air.

"Again that was Chapman," says Tauranac. "Putting them high on stalks made it even more dangerous. You were putting even more loads through the suspension because of the better airflow up there, but you were doing it through structures – the stalks – that were flimsier still. Again we reluctantly followed."

Jochen Rindt, Chapman's leading driver and a man committed to Stewart's safety crusade, saw very clearly the conflict between his own ambitions and his desire for survival. He reckoned wings to be a dangerous development, particularly when allied to Chapman's chancy reputation. Indeed, he and his manager – a small-time racer turned big-ideas businessman called Bernie Ecclestone – viewed his transference to Lotus from Brabham as a calculated risk. They knew he'd be safer at Brabham; they knew he'd be faster, a stronger contender for the title, at Lotus.

Rindt's misgivings about wings and Chapman's design philosophy were vindicated at the 1969 Spanish Grand Prix. No one had been able to calculate the forces going through the various wing stalks and suspensions, but a frightening clue came in this race as both works Lotuses got airborne and crashed when their stalks folded back as they crested the same rise. Rindt and Hill were lucky to escape relatively unharmed, but their copycat accidents forced the sport's governing body to act. Wings were clipped drastically thereafter and Rindt, for one, breathed a sigh of relief. The speed junkies had just been protected from themselves. But clipped or not, what's been invented cannot be uninvented: downforce has been the primary preoccupation of F1 designers ever since.

OPPOSITE: The Honda mechanics experience the pressure of a Grand Prix weekend for the first time as they struggle to make the RA271 race-worthy in time for the 1964 German Grand Prix, the company's F1 debut.

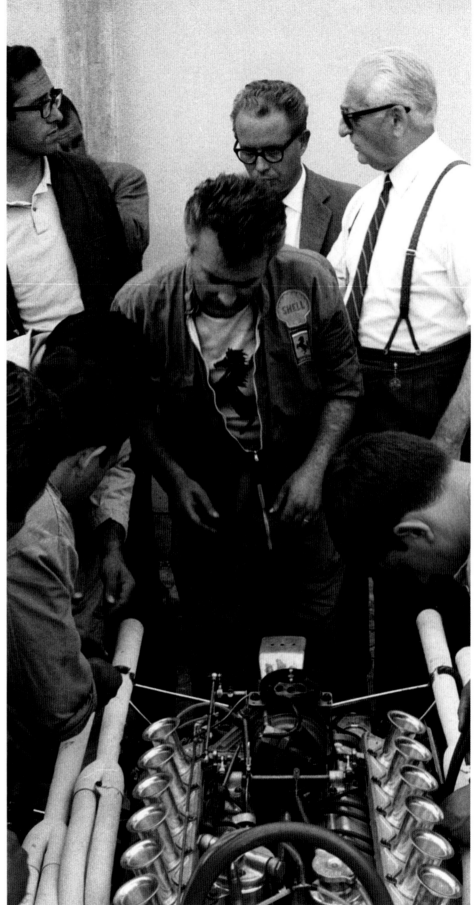

FAR LEFT: Jim Clark sits in the 'bathtub' monocoque of his Lotus 25. The contours of this car had been designed to fit as tightly as possible around the Scot's compact form. Colin Chapman noted: "Even the brake lines beneath the car pass between Jimmy's cheeks!"

MIDDLE LEFT: Enzo Ferrari (far right) fires a question at his chief engineer, a young Mauro Forghieri (far left), across the back of a Ferrari V12 and its 'spaghetti' exhausts. Forghieri has the confidence to look the Old Man square in the eye, a trait that was an essential part of survival under this demanding, autocratic boss. The two men had a tempestuous relationship, but a long one, saying everything about how much Ferrari relied on Forghieri's incredibly versatile talent and workaholic nature.

LEFT: Honda, which arrived in F1 in 1964, did a lot of things very differently to the established European teams. For one thing it introduced corporate clothing for mechanics. John Surtees carried number 14 at Monza in 1967 and '68. He won the first of these – Honda's second Grand Prix victory – and qualified on pole position for the other, only to crash while trying to avoid somebody else's accident.

PREVIOUS SPREAD:

LEFT: Incongruous holiday attire for a 1969 meeting of the Grand Prix Drivers Association at the Kyalami Ranch in South Africa. These are carefree young men whose only job is to drive racing cars, with plenty of downtime to enjoy the sun-kissed locations at which they perform. But there is a downside: the regular culling of their number. This shot encapsulates the contrast. The GPDA was the leading body pushing for safety improvements. Louis Stanley (in jacket), the team principal of BRM and a significant contributor to the safety crusade, is chairing the meeting. Sitting centre stage is Jochen Rindt. In front of him, with his back to the camera, is Jacky Ickx. Between them, mainly obscured, is Jackie Stewart. Ickx would later disassociate himself from the GPDA and was critical of Stewart's campaign. Today, distant from his racer's addiction, Ickx recognises that he probably owes his life to Stewart. On Rindt's left are 1967 world champion Denny Hulme and new kid on the block Mario Andretti. On Rindt's right are Chris Amon and, with his back partially to camera, the 1962 and '68 world champion Graham Hill. Lying between them is Jean-Pierre Beltoise.

RIGHT: While the drivers were working out how their addiction could be made safer, the constructors were going through a phase when their own competitive addiction was making the cars much more dangerous. Lotus took the suspension-mounted wing to new and perilous heights here at Brands Hatch in 1968.

ABOVE: **BRM mechanics use lateral thinking. The underside of this car is typical of any late-1960s F1 machine. The only concession to aerodynamics is to have the underside enclosed (apart from around the engine area because of cooling needs) to reduce drag. In time designers would come to realise that the harnessing of underbody airflow to provide downforce was the key to massive performance increases.**

RIGHT: **Jim Clark confers with Colin Chapman during the 1964 Dutch Grand Prix. The Lotus 25 was by now on lower-profile Dunlops than the year before. Shallower, stiffer sidewalls meant that the tyre flexed less, allowing the suspension to be more efficient.**

LEFT: A high-speed mix of talent, image and professionalism: Jackie Stewart's Matra MS80 blasts by at Clermont-Ferrand during the 1969 French Grand Prix, a race the Scot led from start to finish. The identity of the late Jim Clark's natural successor becomes yet clearer. Of Stewart's generation, Jochen Rindt and Chris Amon were the other obvious contenders but neither had got themselves into settled competitive environments: Rindt was in his first season with Lotus and rowing frequently with team boss Colin Chapman about the safety and reliability of his cars; Amon was hampered by an uncompetitive Ferrari and his next career move wasn't clear.

ABOVE: Denny Hulme's defence of his world title came to an end shortly after this photograph was taken, his McLaren's 1968 Mexican Grand Prix ending with a broken gearbox output shaft. With only one rear wheel being driven as he accelerated out of a corner, the car spun and sent Hulme crashing into a culvert formed by a ditch and an access road. Investigation of the component suggested a fatigue failure and the design was subsequently modified. The test pilot aspect of the F1 driver's job was still very evident.

FOLLOWING SPREAD: Villagers watch as the 1964 Belgian Grand Prix screams past their houses on the public roads of Spa-Francorchamps. The man in a blurry rush is Dan Gurney. He dominated the race from pole position, recording the fastest lap in the process, and looked set for a convincing win until his Brabham BT7 ran out of fuel on the last lap. Jim Clark's Lotus 25 ran out of petrol too, albeit on the slowing-down lap, and the pair of them were chatting by the side of the track when the public address system announced Clark as the (surprised) winner.

1961 – NEW FORMULA

MAXIMUM ENGINE CAPACITY: 1.5 litres normally aspirated; 1.3 litres with forced induction.

1962 – MONOCOQUE CONSTRUCTION

Yet another idea first embraced in aircraft manufacture, the monocoque was a load-bearing shell that made the previous complex arrangements of tubing obsolete. Now the body *was* the chassis, not merely something that was bolted onto it. This made its F1 debut on the Lotus 25 (top left). As well as simplifying the structure of the car, the 25's monocoque was three times stiffer and half the weight of the space frame of the concurrent F1 Lotus 24. The stiffer a chassis the more loadings it is able to take and the more accurately its suspension can be controlled.

Robin Read was an employee of Lotus boss Colin Chapman at the time the 25 was conceived. He explains what drove the idea: "There were a number of motives. Colin didn't like the restrictions of a space frame – it had to have lots of holes in the wrong places – and a small frontal area imposed very complicated fuel-tanking arrangements that were continually splitting and leaking. There was nothing terribly original about a monocoque; it was used extensively in aircraft and even the centre section of the [three-time Le Mans winner of the 1950s] D-type Jaguar was very close to the sort of technology used on the 25. It's just that Colin did it in such a blindingly obvious way. I can distinctly remember him saying all you need is a fuel tank, an engine, a gearbox, four wheels and a driver. It was obvious when we saw it coming together that he really had something, that it was brilliant. Those cars with the 1.5-litre engines were very lightly stressed compared with what would come."

Mike Costin, then a Lotus director, adds: "Colin outlined it to us at Waltham Cross. We used to go there for lunch sometimes and he drew the principle on a napkin. You could say that all he did was replace all that tubing with two bloody great tubes – but even so, the section modulus goes up enormously; if you double the cross-sectional area of a tube you make it 16 times as stiff."

With stiffer chassis and advances in rubber compounding came ever-wider tyres: sizes went from 6.5 inches in 1960 to 14 by '69. Cornering speeds increased accordingly.

1966 – NEW FORMULA

MAXIMUM ENGINE CAPACITY: 3 litres normally aspirated; 1.5 litres with forced induction.

1967 – FORD-COSWORTH DFV ENGINE

With the arrival of the 3-litre formula came the chance to conceive and build an F1 power plant from scratch. Lotus had a strong working relationship in the lower formulae with engine-builder Cosworth, whose co-founder and designer Keith Duckworth had once been a Lotus employee. Chapman and Duckworth discussed an engine that would be a stressed part of the car's structure, further increasing chassis stiffness. Chapman had already done this in 1966 with the BRM H16 engine in his Lotus 43 – but the new engine was to be the antithesis of the H16: light, simple and compact. Sponsored by Ford, the resultant Cosworth DFV V8 (top right) was a masterpiece.

Cosworth co-founder Costin recalls the uneasy relationship between Chapman and Duckworth: "When Keith worked at Lotus they didn't get on well together, there was no accepting of each other. Later on, when Keith was established and successful, Colin was wary of him because he didn't want to upset him.

"Colin was a very good conceptual engineer. He understood structures and materials but sometimes allowed himself the luxury of illogicality. It's very difficult to force yourself to see every step of the design of a mechanism. Failures occur, generally due to an illogical step taken by an engineer at the design stage. It's a sin of omission, i.e. not making yourself think of every step. A step missed is a wrong step. That was the difference between Chapman and Duckworth – Keith would never allow himself an illogical step."

Installed in the back of the new Lotus 49, the DFV won on its debut in the 1967 Dutch Grand Prix, with Jim Clark at its wheel. Later released to other teams on a commercial basis, it would become the most successful F1 engine of all time, racking up Grands Prix wins over a 15-year period. Having F1's best engine generally available allowed the independent 'kit car' constructors established in Cooper's wake to thrive.

1968 – WINGS

The principle of turning an aircraft wing-shape upside down to create downforce as opposed to lift had been sporadically applied to racing cars over the years, but never to F1 cars. But it was a development that, once released, would provide a massive performance boost (bottom left).

1969 – LIMITING OF WINGS

Some lethal developments followed the first fumbling steps towards downforce. F1 was venturing into uncharted and dangerous waters, and after two copycat crashes caused by wing failures at the Spanish Grand Prix, F1's new addenda were banned outright at the next race. A compromise was subsequently reached with the constructors whereby the wings could stay – but only if they were drastically limited in height, immovable and *not* mounted to the suspension.

Within these new limitations, the Lotus 72 of 1970 (bottom right) partly resolved the conflicting requirements of downforce and drag with a wedge-shaped body that created a small measure of its own downforce and so allowed smaller wings for the same downward thrust – to the benefit of straight-line speed.

Mr. Big

Immediately he heard the news, Bernie Ecclestone began running, as fast as he could, from the Monza pits to the Parabolica turn. But by the time he got there Jochen Rindt had already been carried from the wreckage of his Lotus 72 to an ambulance. Ecclestone forlornly picked up his friend's helmet, a shoe and a wheel with parts of suspension still attached. Inside the ambulance, doctors fought to save Rindt's life.

Rindt and his manager Ecclestone had been right after all: Lotus had offered him a better chance than Brabham of the world title – no one overhauled Rindt's 1970 points tally in the four races that remained – but there had been a very real risk attached. His title was posthumous, his injuries too great for the doctors to combat.

This had happened to Ecclestone before. Back in 1958 he had been managing the career of close friend Stuart Lewis-Evans when the driver suffered fatal burns in a crash at the Moroccan Grand Prix. A devastated Ecclestone had left the sport for a few years after that, only gradually drifting back. This time, though, he stayed around and bought into the Brabham team in the wake of Jack Brabham selling up and retiring. The sport reverberates still to the consequences of this.

The other team owners were racing junkies, who, if they had any business sense, used it simply to feed their habit. Ecclestone's addiction was business, and he was brilliantly adept at it. Motor racing was a side order – at least it was until he saw the huge money-making opportunities there. It took someone of his vision to recognize them, but they were there. In a commercial sense, F1 was Wild West territory, drastically underdeveloped and with huge future rewards on offer for those with the gumption to stake their claim early.

Although the teams had sponsorship, Ecclestone saw that the sport had hardly begun to capitalise on the concept. Instead of fighting each other over their share of a small cake, he thought in terms of a bigger cake, with television its prime ingredient.

But that was a long-term aim. First off, a bit of housekeeping: he set about tidying the archaic way the sport went about its business. No longer would teams individually bargain with race promoters for their fees. Instead Ecclestone banded them together and, as their sole representative, offered the circuits a take-it-or-leave-it package. The spoils would then be shared out among the teams based on merit. In effect, Ecclestone became the series' promoter. The team owners, relieved at having someone else bear the burden of thinking about macro-business (the sport) as opposed to micro- (their own teams), gave Ecclestone carte blanche to represent their interests, leaving them in peace to make their

Unlike the others, Bernie Ecclestone wasn't addicted to the sport, but to business. His vision in the early 1970s led him to see F1 as wild west territory, with huge future rewards on offer for those who staked their claim.

ever-faster machines. He would make them very rich in the process, but himself vastly more so – the prize of the entrepreneur.

There was a critical moment of stand-off during 1975 as the Canadian Grand Prix's organisers attempted to beat down Ecclestone's late-notice race fee increase. Their chief, Bob Hanna, was quoted as saying: "The future of Grand Prix rests in the fact that this little group [the F1 Constructors Association] has to be broken up." Ecclestone informed the Canadian organisers that his members wouldn't be coming if the extra fee wasn't paid. He gave them a deadline. It passed, and Ecclestone's office issued a press release stating the race was off. The organisers relented and agreed to pay. Ecclestone gathered the constructors together and suggested that they still didn't go, on account of the deadline having been and gone. The constructors initially disagreed until one of their number – March's Max Mosley – turned up to the meeting late and eloquently changed their minds. The race did not go ahead. With some help from Mosley, the balance of power had just shifted decisively in Ecclestone's favour. It was a key moment in Bernie staking his territorial claim to the sport.

Coming on top of Stewart's safety demands, the circuit owners didn't like it. Nor did a governing body that was largely comprised of old-money blue bloods with little feel for the commercial realities

of a quickly changing world. The sport was threatening to leave them behind.

Stewart had been a close friend of Rindt's and was on the scene as they tried to save him from his terrible injuries. This was the third of his F1 colleagues killed in 1970 alone. He later told Heinz Prüller, Rindt's biographer, what he went through as he next climbed into his car: "As I put on my helmet the tears started rolling. I went back into my pit in order to regain control over myself; then I climbed into the car. While the mechanics strapped me in I started crying again, but no one saw it because I was wearing my helmet and mask. But when the engine came to life, and when I drove off, I was aware of only one sensation: I tasted salt." Racing past the scene of Rindt's demise, Stewart continued, "It was a different Stewart who glanced to the left and thought, 'So that's the spot'. This other Stewart was completely without feelings, without emotion; nothing existed inside him. Now I wanted to drive as fast as I could, not because I needed to assert myself over the car, or my fear or my feelings, but because I didn't want to stay in the car for long; the faster I drove, the sooner I could get out. As I drove my fastest practice time, I felt an odd sort of satisfaction. But when I stopped, my eyes were moist again."

It can be a perverse sport. A normal human being might stop

LEFT: Lotus boss Colin Chapman celebrates Emerson Fittipaldi's title-clinching win at the 1972 Italian Grand Prix in characteristic fashion: hurling his cap high.

MIDDLE: Fittipaldi enjoyed a two-year stint at McLaren, winning the team's first world championship in 1974. He had left Lotus after being outpaced by team-mate Ronnie Peterson.

RIGHT: Jochen Rindt on the Hockenheim podium after his final Grand Prix victory, August 2, 1970. He would never know it, but he had just secured the world championship.

after being so close to such catastrophe. Most racers acknowledged fate when they were outside the car, assumed it was only for others when in it. Stewart went eyeball to eyeball with reality and set about changing it with yet more resolve.

Stewart wanted to stay alive, Ecclestone wanted to make money – but where that pulled the sport was merely of the time.If it hadn't been them it would've been someone else. It was time. Just as the discovery of downforce had completed the five fundamental parameters of performance – power, weight, tyre grip, drag and downforce – so commercialisation was F1's final link in the chain. Everything that has followed has been just more of the same. The late 1960s and early '70s were when the final philosophical frontiers were broken. It made the sport a smaller field of endeavour, lost it some of its grandeur, but its popularity, and therefore its appeal to commercial entities, guaranteed this was its fate, good or bad.

Death has the ultimate hold on western thought; we spend our lives afraid of its approach. But there's a suspicion that life is extra vivid out there right on the edge, taunting death, spurning it. That's what lent the matadors, mountaineers and racing drivers their fascination. But bullfighting and mountaineering remain pure because they don't interest corporations, don't get beamed across

the globe, haven't been embraced by the modern world. A sport like F1, based so heavily on technology, was never going to be immune from that world.

It was still racing, still the ultimate form of it – and because technology still lagged behind intent in terms of safety, for a time it retained a raw edge. But now F1 was showbiz and shop window, too. Ecclestone enticed the TV companies, who liked the advertising revenue that went with the viewing figures, and then ramped up the terms. And still they paid, happily. With global TV coverage exploding, the sponsors came running. Meanwhile, the core participants just did what they'd always done: raced.

They gave Ecclestone some great storylines to help him in his quest. As if the return of Ferrari – one of the most recognised and prestigious brands in the world, the jewel in F1's crown – to world championship glory in 1975 after an 11-year drought wasn't enough, the following year was even better. First, someone invented a six-wheel car; the Tyrrell P34 wasn't any faster than the best four-wheelers but it captured the imagination of the outside world. But not half as much as the startling title battle that raged between McLaren's James Hunt and Ferrari's Niki Lauda.

OPPOSITE: Jody Scheckter celebrates winning the 1977 Argentinian Grand Prix, a remarkable achievement given that he was driving for Wolf, a brand-new team. He went on to finish runner-up in that year's title race after taking two more wins: Monaco and Canada.

Bruce McLaren in his eponymous M14A on his way to finishing second in the 1970 Spanish Grand Prix. It was to be his penultimate F1 race. A few weeks later he was killed testing a Can-Am McLaren at Goodwood. As an F1 driver he was good but not great. As an inspirational team leader he was very special. His mellow disposition hid a fierce determination and, according to his one-time designer Robin Herd, "He had a charisma that just magically drew extraordinary people around him." His early career benefited from the assistance of Jack Brabham. Journalist Eoin Young, a close friend of McLaren's, said: "In the early days Jack Brabham would go out to Australia and New Zealand with the Coopers he'd been racing all year in Europe and sell them to the McLaren family, whom he looked upon as a sort of willing chequebook. Bruce in turn was fortunate that Jack was a bit of a loner and saw Bruce as a good understudy, the ideal number two, a driver who wasn't ever going to beat him in a straight fight."

ABOVE: James Hunt's McLaren M23 gets airborne in the opening seconds of the 1977 United States Grand Prix West after attempting to chop across the front of John Watson's Brabham BT45B-Alfa Romeo. Ronnie Peterson's Tyrrell P34B – the right-rear wheel of which can just be seen beneath the McLaren – has to go straight on to avoid colliding with Hunt and loses many places as a result. "James was terrific when he could get in clean air," says Watson, "but he was pretty awful if he had to get through traffic." In fairness, this clash was actually triggered by Carlos Reutemann locking-up his Ferrari's brakes and running wide, forcing Watson and Hunt to dive for the same piece of racetrack.

RIGHT: Jody Scheckter leads Patrick Depailler in a Tyrrell 1-2 at the 1974 Swedish Grand Prix. South African Scheckter was a thrusting, natural-born winner. His talent was directed by a shrewd, almost cynical intelligence. He knew what he wanted from the sport, and if his push to achieve it was often less than delicate, it was invariably effective. This was the scene of his first Grand Prix victory. Five years later he would achieve his aim of the world championship. One year after that, he would retire a rich man, aged just 30. Rarely, if ever, has a driver been able to control his addiction so effectively. His career was like a military operation: in, capture, out. By contrast, his team-mate Depailler was a man hopelessly in love with the sport, unable even to envisage how he could ever leave, other than in a box. Yet when it came to it, Scheckter's driven ambition took him more readily to areas of necessary risk than Depailler's romanticism. Depailler's long-time friend Jean-Paul Ray recalled: "Patrick was honest enough to admit to me that he was a bit afraid. He said it was very pleasurable to drive maybe two-tenths off, but to find those two-tenths was not nice, not comfortable." At this race the Tyrrell 007s had qualified 1-2, with Depailler on pole, neither man having yet won a Grand Prix. Team boss Ken Tyrrell instructed that whichever of them got ahead at the start would stay in front and the other would remain in a support role. With so much at stake there was never going to be any contest: Scheckter scorched into the lead at the first corner, Depailler fell back to third. Six years later, Depailler left F1 the way he always accepted he might.

LEFT: Graham Hill, 46 years old at the beginning of 1975, was considering finally stepping out of the cockpit to concentrate on running the team he'd created in 1973. His driving skills were considerably dimmed by this time, but the fierce determination that had been such a central part of his success during the 1960s prevented him from hanging up his helmet earlier. He announced his retirement at the British Grand Prix and received a standing ovation from the Silverstone crowd. Four months later he was killed when the plane he was piloting crashed in fog as he attempted to land at Elstree airfield. His lead driver, designer and team manager were also killed, and this promising team was swiftly wound up.

TOP RIGHT: Franco's *guardia* watch over Ronnie Peterson's Lotus 72E during the 1975 Spanish Grand Prix, the last to be held at Montjuich Park. The event was cursed. It began with a big row between the teams and organisers when it was discovered that agreed safety precautions had not been made. The teams were ready to refuse to take part; the organisers threatened to impound their cars and stationed police on the paddock exits to prevent them leaving. The race went ahead.

BOTTOM RIGHT: Emerson Fittipaldi struggled to finish eighth as reigning world champion in the 1975 Swedish Grand Prix. The high airbox of his McLaren M23 was very much a standard design feature of F1 cars of the period. It forced air into the engine at a higher pressure than the atmosphere by slowing down its flow, giving a slight supercharged effect. The governing body considered the airboxes unsightly and drastically cut their dimensions early in the 1976 season.

ABOVE: Mario Andretti – here celebrating victory in the 1977 United States Grand Prix West at Long Beach – dreamed of being a racing driver as a child in Italy. Those dreams were apparently shattered when his family moved to the USA – until he discovered they raced cars there, too. After an apprenticeship served on dirt tracks and ovals, he was already one of the most accomplished and versatile racers around when he received his F1 opportunity at the end of 1968. He put his Lotus 49B on pole position on his Grand Prix debut, but didn't commit fully to F1 until 1976, having won the 1971 South African Grand Prix for Ferrari in the meantime. He was instrumental in Lotus regaining its competitive drive in 1976 and won the final race of that year, Japan. Equipped with the ground effect Lotus 78 and 79 models, he scored 10 further wins during the next two seasons and became the world champion in 1978. His final full F1 season was with Alfa Romeo in 1981. But he scored a heroic pole position at Monza as a stand-in Ferrari driver in 1982, and continued racing his beloved American Champcars until 1994.

RIGHT: The six-wheeled Tyrrell P34 of 1976 – seen here at Watkins Glen – won the Swedish Grand Prix of that year in Jody Scheckter's hands. But the South African racer was not a fan of the car: "The idea was that with more rubber on the ground it would be better under braking, and that with less drag from four small wheels it would be faster down the straights. But, for me, those things never translated. The braking advantage disappeared once you locked-up one of those little wheels and all the others promptly locked-up, too. As for the straights, we did some back-to-back tests with the old four-wheel Tyrrell and the six-wheeler was slightly quicker – but they were running it with less wing!"

Tyres dancing on the edge of adhesion, throttle foot to the floor, spirit soaring high into a clear Spanish sky: Jacky Ickx lives out the dream in his Lotus 76 at Jarama in 1974. But there was something missing. It isn't usually age that catches up with a driver but a dwindling of his desire. Wringing the last few tenths out of a car causes the risk factor to go exponential. A man has to be almost insanely driven to routinely go into that territory, but that is what F1 demands of a driver. Since his F1 debut in 1967 Ickx's performances had been characterised by a very clear willingness to expose himself to risk. Maybe that burned him out, because by 1974 he was beginning to lose his addiction and was slowing. At just 29, he was perhaps the youngest has-been F1 had ever seen. He continued his career, extremely successfully, in the less demanding category of endurance racing for a further 11 years.

The Monza *tifosi* enjoy their traditional post-race track invasion. This is 1973 – but even today the fans still invade the circuit. The big difference is that the modern race organiser is rather better at ensuring that the racing has actually finished before the floodgates are opened. The situation is similar at Italy's other F1 track, Imola, where in 1983 Bruno Giacomelli took seventh place off Nigel Mansell on the final run to the line when Mansell lifted off to avoid the fans, and Giacomelli didn't.

TOP LEFT: Big boost gauge to the left, central rev-counter – that's about all you had time for in an F1 turbo car. René Arnoux took 18 poles during this era and remembers the chaos of a qualifying lap: "You were running the boost much higher than at any other time, plus you had new qualifying tyres that worked for only one lap. So you had much more power and much more grip than you'd tried the car with before – but you still had to do it over just one lap. It was a big, crazy blur. You were just reacting and trying to get on the gas as early as you could. In later cars there was a button you could press that got you even more boost for a short burst and you were just trying to hit this button as often as possible during the lap in between getting bounced and banged around. You really couldn't remember much about it afterwards."

BOTTOM LEFT: As a response to the dominance of the ground effect Lotus 79 of 1978, Brabham produced the BT46/2 'fan car' in time for the Swedish Grand Prix. Taking his cue from the Chaparral 2J sports-racer, Brabham's designer Gordon Murray sectioned-off the rear underside of the car and used an engine-driven fan to suck it down to the ground. He got around the ban on moveable aerodynamic devices (in place since moveable wings were outlawed in 1969) by saying any aerodynamic effect was unintentional and that the primary purpose of the fan was for cooling! The car dominated the race, Niki Lauda and John Watson scoring a 1-2. Fellow constructors were in uproar and Brabham boss Bernie Ecclestone agreed that the car would not be raced again. "That car was going to be just the

beginning," reveals Murray. "We were already working on the next stage, a very-square-cross-section, variable-pitch fan car, the BT47, which would have been a big leap forward."

RIGHT: Peter Revson sits inside his unclothed McLaren. Son of the co-founder of Revlon Cosmetics, he fought fierce family antipathy to pursue a career on his own terms, and received no financial help from them. He was the racing driver on Hollywood's A-list: handsome, debonair, filling the social pages and dating Miss World. But the sophistication endemic to his monied New York upbringing hid an incredible grit. He served a long racing apprenticeship: his first Grand Prix was in 1964 and it wasn't until 1973 that he finally established himself as a genuine world-class performer. He won two races that year: Britain and Canada. He viewed his salary as an index of his worth as a racing driver and it was perhaps this skewed view that caused him to leave McLaren, spurn a Ferrari offer and instead join Shadow for 1974. He was killed while testing for the South African Grand Prix. His friend and biographer Leon Mandell said: "It was all about money, which is some irony considering the family we're dealing with. It was the wrong strategic move, the wrong tactical move, the wrong career move – and it ended as it inevitably had to end."

FAR RIGHT: Even though he'd never previously won a Grand Prix, when Revson saw the odds at Silverstone in 1973 – they were even longer at the time, 14-to-1 – he placed a £50 bet on himself. He wasn't totally confident, though, and went each way, not on the nose. Which is a shame – because he won!

BELOW: Ferrari mechanics in 1977. The fact that their shirts are immaculate says everything about the excellence of their cars' reliability of that year. Notice that one of them has a 'F1CA' badge. This was the original moniker of the F1 Constructors Association – until someone pointed out that *fica* sounded like something quite rude in Italian. The abbreviation was thereafter changed to 'FOCA' – which sounds like something quite rude in English!

RIGHT: Facilities were still rudimentary in 1974, even though teams' commercial incomes were on a steep rise. McLaren and Tyrrell – both potential champions that season – are forced to share a garage.

LEFT: The first lap of the 1977 Monaco Grand Prix. Leader Jody Scheckter's Wolf WR1 is already out of shot as second-placed John Watson's Brabham BT45B-Alfa Romeo heads Carlos Reutemann's Ferrari 312T2, Hans Stuck's Brabham, Ronnie Peterson's Tyrrell P34B, Niki Lauda's Ferrari, James Hunt's McLaren M23, Patrick Depailler's Tyrrell, Mario Andretti's Lotus 78, Jochen Mass's McLaren, Alan Jones's Shadow DN8, Jean-Pierre Jarier's ATS-Penske PC4, Gunnar Nilsson's Lotus, Riccardo Patrese's Shadow, Vittorio Brambilla's Surtees TS19, Jacques Laffite's Ligier JS7, Jacky Ickx's Ensign N177 and Emerson Fittipaldi's Copersucar FD04.None of them were able to catch Scheckter.

RIGHT: Roger Williamson perished in this fiery accident at the 1973 Dutch Grand Prix. David Purley parked his privateer March 731 on the opposite side of the track and ran over to Williamson's aid. He tried to right the upturned works March and pleaded with the shocked marshals to help him, grabbing an extinguisher from one of them. Purley received the George Medal for this act of bravery – but it was no consolation for the loss of his friend. Purley would survive a much more violent impact at Silverstone in 1977, only to be killed in an aerobatics biplane eight years later.

FOLLOWING SPREAD:

LEFT: The aftermath of the crash that occurred seconds after the start of the 1978 Italian Grand Prix. The cars of James Hunt, Ronnie Peterson, Clay Regazzoni and Vittorio Brambilla litter the scene as Peterson (lying on a stretcher on the track) and Brambilla (in the car alongside the barriers) receive medical attention. Peterson had received a broken leg and Brambilla a serious head injury from a bouncing wheel. Peterson later died in hospital from an embolism triggered by the broken bone; Brambilla made a slow but full recovery.

RIGHT: Shade and light form a beautiful image of a beautiful circuit as François Cevert (Tyrrell 006) fights with Emerson Fittipaldi (Lotus 72E) at Montjuich Park during the 1973 Spanish Grand Prix. Strips of darkened rubber on three of Cevert's tyres show that he is already struggling with wear; he would later pit for a new set of Goodyears. Fittipaldi meanwhile rose to the front of the field and stayed there despite a slowly deflating rear tyre. With magical delicacy he somehow kept it all together to take a superbly judged victory, the tyre all but flat by the end. Cevert recovered from his early stop to finish runner-up.

TOP LEFT: The barrister and the car dealer. Two clever misfits, Max Mosley and Bernie Ecclestone, washed up in F1 in the 1970s and have since guided it to global domination.

BOTTOM LEFT: Former team-mates Graham Hill and Jackie Stewart share some good-natured banter as they sport their 1970s hairstyles. Stewart used to refer to Hill as 'Pop', deliberately emphasising the 10-year age difference between them.

RIGHT: Ken Tyrrell doesn't want to hear about Bernie Ecclestone's latest business deals. He just wants to go racing. It was an attitude he would later rethink.

FAR RIGHT: James Hunt about to try an experimental bib spoiler on his Hesketh 308 in practice for the 1975 German Grand Prix. Lord Alexander Hesketh (far right) is maybe pondering how this is all costing more money than he cares to spend. He drastically cut back the operation the following year, and pulled out completely early in 1978.

TOP LEFT: The view the front row had of the John Player grid girls at the 1973 British Grand Prix. As one of the last bastions of male dominance, F1 tended to use women only for adornment.

BELOW LEFT: The Goodyear service area in the Zolder paddock at the 1973 Belgian Grand Prix. The Ohio-based company had by this time asserted itself over Firestone and would soon find itself the monopoly tyre supplier to F1.

RIGHT: Brake discs inboard of the suspension was a development F1 courted through much of the 1970s. It reduced unsprung weight and therefore theoretically increased grip, but there were definite downsides: the shafts connecting the brake to the wheel tended to fail, while the (usually) useful side effect of a disc radiating heat directly into a tyre had now been removed from the equation.

FOLLOWING SPREAD:
LEFT: Jacky Ickx's Ferrari 312B leads the 1970 British Grand Prix at Brands Hatch as Jochen Rindt squeezes his Lotus 72 past the Brabham BT33 of his former team boss Jack Brabham at Paddock Hill Bend. Ickx retired with a broken differential after seven laps,

leaving Rindt out front. But with 11 laps to go – and under pressure from Brabham – Rindt made a mistake at Clearways that allowed Jack to repass. Entering the final lap Brabham was comfortably ahead – but ran out of fuel approaching the last corner, allowing Rindt to steal the win. Brabham mechanic Nick Goozée had mistakenly left the car's fuel metering on its full-rich setting after the warm-up lap. Goozée's colleague Ron Dennis moved towards the car after the race and was seen by Brabham, who, assuming it had been Dennis who'd committed the error, ordered him to leave everything just as it was. For decades it was widely believed that Dennis, who subsequently became McLaren's team boss, had cost Brabham the race. Dennis loyally retained his silence and Goozée finally came clean 33 years later, after retiring from his position as chairman of Penske Cars.

RIGHT: Jody Scheckter raced in the early part of 1974 in the retired Jackie Stewart's '73 title-winning Tyrrell 006. However, its short wheelbase made for nervous handling that the relatively inexperienced Scheckter disliked.

LEFT: The remarkable McLaren M23, here at the 1976 Austrian Grand Prix, took James Hunt to the world title of that season, three years after its debut. This longevity not only illustrated the quality of Gordon Coppuck's design but also the stagnant technical period that F1 was then passing through.

RIGHT: A crowd surrounds Patrick Depailler's Tyrrell P34 at Paul Ricard. The car has been left unattended in a spectator enclosure adjacent to the paddock during practice for the 1976 French Grand Prix. In contrast, the current F1 teams go to great lengths at races to prevent outsiders from getting close to their cars.

TOP LEFT: Jack Brabham, Andrea de Adamich, Rolf Stommelen, Peter Gethin (with an impassive Denny Hulme's fingers providing devil's horns!), Henri Pescarolo, Hulme, an obscured Ronnie Peterson and Jean-Pierre Beltoise are all smiles before the 1970 Canadian Grand Prix, no doubt putting to the back of their minds the fact that yet another of their peers, Jochen Rindt, had been killed just three weeks earlier.

BOTTOM LEFT: Ken Tyrrell in conference with his 1977 drivers, Ronnie Peterson and Patrick Depailler, neither of whom could make the six-wheeler competitive that year.

RIGHT: Modern F1 steering wheels have long since surrendered their circular form in order that drivers can pass their legs underneath them in cockpits made ever-tighter by the need to reduce drag. This McLaren, however, provides a particularly early take on the idea. The red line on the Smiths rev-counter is a 'tell-tale'. It indicated the maximum rpm a driver had used on his most recent run in the car.

ABOVE: The 1970 German Grand Prix gets under way in an explosion of noise and colour, with layer upon layer of fans crammed into Hockenheim's huge grandstands. From left at the front are Pedro Rodriguez (white BRM P153), Jo Siffert (March 701), Chris Amon (March 701), Jochen Rindt (Lotus 72), and the Ferrari 312Bs of Clay Regazzoni and Jacky Ickx. Rindt would win – his final victory – after a battle with Ickx. The race was held at Hockenheim because the Nürburgring was undergoing a refit.

RIGHT: Jochen Rindt on his way to his final Grand Prix victory, Hockenheim 1970. The beautiful but fragile Lotus 72 gifted Rindt the consistent success that had previously seemed elusive despite a startling talent. During the 1970 season he was even winning 'lucky' races, where others fell out ahead of him. It was as if the waves of fortune had finally turned in his favour, but it was a cruel deception. He was arguing with himself about whether to retire at the end of the season if, as seemed likely, he were to win the world championship. The decision was taken out of his hands just over a month after this picture, with his death during practice for the Italian Grand Prix.

TOP ROW:

LEFT: Ronnie Peterson and Colin Chapman, both geniuses in their respective fields, worked together in 1973-76 and again in 1978. Peterson could 'bend' a car to his will to an extraordinary degree but lacked technical nous. He excelled when teamed with a technically minded driver, such as Emerson Fittipaldi in 1973 or Mario Andretti in 1978.

MIDDLE: Jackie Stewart talks the press around the Watkins Glen track on the eve of the 1973 American Grand Prix. This race was due to be his 100th – and last – Grand Prix start, but he withdrew after the death of François Cevert, his Tyrrell team-mate, in qualifying.

RIGHT: Ronnie Peterson (March 721G) leads Jacky Ickx (Ferrari 312B2) in the 1972 American Grand Prix at Watkins Glen. Peterson had crashed in practice, an occurrence that restricted him to 26th position on the grid. But during the race he charged with characteristic commitment to finish fourth, passing Ickx along the way. The 721G was an F2 car hastily converted to F1 specification after the intended F1 model – 721X – proved slow. The crudity of the conversion, with its enlarged radiators and plumbing standing proud of the compact bodywork, is very evident here.

BOTTOM ROW:

LEFT: Bernie Ecclestone, in his guise as a team owner, recruited Niki Lauda to drive for Brabham in 1978 and '79. The two men hit it off, and the incumbent driver John Watson received a lesson in leadership from Lauda: "He just came in, and without explicitly saying anything, simply took over as the lead driver. I didn't feel he could drive any quicker than me; it was simply the force of his personality. I would come in during qualifying and ask for my qualifying tyres, only to find Niki had taken them. He created an energy around him and suddenly everything was focused on him."

MIDDLE: Handling characteristics: Emerson Fittipaldi's Lotus 72 oversteers and Jackie Stewart's Tyrrell 005 understeers around one

of the Österreichring's 150mph bends. Stewart led the 1972 Austrian Grand Prix for 23 laps but finally succumbed to Fittipaldi's pressure – and handling problems that finally restricted him to seventh place. Fittipaldi won, and his first world title was now within reach.

RIGHT: The Österreichring's magnificent mountain setting. The track hosted the Austrian Grand Prix between 1970 and '87. This is 1974. In scorching August heat, Carlos Reutemann's Brabham BT44 led throughout.

FOLLOWING SPREAD:

LEFT: Niki Lauda sits in a 1974 Ferrari 312B3 early in his remarkable F1 career. Born into a wealthy Viennese family that resolutely opposed his racing, he took out a bank loan to fund his early career, using nothing other than his family's good name as collateral. Despite ever-mounting debts, he paid for his first F1 season, 1972, the plan being to establish himself in order that he could command a salary the following year. He suffered a mediocre season and, with his plan apparently in tatters, briefly considered suicide. Instead he simply upped the stakes with more fast and loose double-dealing that landed him a drive with BRM for 1973. This time he performed, showing such promise that he was recruited by Ferrari for 1974 – and saved from financial ruin. His rare analytical skills and neat, efficient driving mixed well with Ferrari's test facilities and chief engineer Mauro Forghieri. They took one another to the heights of the world championship in 1975. Lauda was almost killed in a fiery accident at the 1976 German Grand Prix but staged a remarkable recovery that culminated in his second world title in 1977. He retired for the first time at the end of 1979 and built up his own airline, but after two years away made a comeback with McLaren. He won his third race back and in 1984 secured his third title. He retired for good at the end of 1985.

RIGHT: Ferrari fans find a novel use for an Agip advertising hoarding at Monza.

Jean-Pierre Jarier crashed his Shadow DN5 out of the 1975 British Grand Prix. In common with Carlos Pace, Jody Scheckter, James Hunt, Mark Donohue, Jochen Mass, Patrick Depailler, John Watson, Tony Brise, Brian Henton, John Nicholson, Dave Morgan, Wilson Fittipaldi, Tom Pryce and Hans Stuck, he had been caught out by a sudden downpour.

TOP LEFT: **Ronnie Peterson and Mario Andretti, pictured late in 1977 – shortly after the announcement that Peterson would be rejoining Lotus alongside the American star. Despite the friendliness, Mario was less than amused that a driver of Ronnie's calibre should be given the opportunity to benefit from all the work he had put in to make Lotus competitive again. "Tell me where it says there should be two prima donnas in a team," said Andretti. He needn't have worried – Peterson stayed true to a stipulated 'number two' role in his contract during 1978. This is an extremely challenging situation for a racing driver, but it was one that Peterson accepted in exchange for getting in a car that was fast enough to relaunch his career after a few quiet seasons.**

BOTTOM LEFT: **Backgammon was the game of choice in the F1 paddock during the less pressured times of the 1970s. James Hunt (left) pits his wits.**

RIGHT: **Denny Hulme's McLaren M19A during the 1971 French Grand Prix at Paul Ricard. It would retire with ignition problems.**

LEFT: **Gilles Villeneuve suffers a puncture on his Ferrari 312T3 during practice for the 1978 Belgian Grand Prix. In the race he was the only man able to pressure the much faster ground effect Lotus 79 of Mario Andretti. Yet this was only Villeneuve's first full season in F1.**

TOP RIGHT: **James Hunt fights to defend his lead from Carlos Reutemann's Ferrari 312T2 in the 1977 Brazilian Grand Prix. Reutemann eventually passed the Brit to win, with Hunt's McLaren M23 second. Reutemann would win the following year's Brazilian race, too; this time, though, it was held at Rio not Interlagos, and his Ferrari was on Michelin tyres not Goodyears. This was the first F1 win for the French company's radial construction.**

BOTTOM RIGHT: **Mario Andretti's Lotus 78 laps Jochen Mass's McLaren M23 during the 1977 French Grand Prix. The Lotus represented a major technological leap forward from previous-generation cars like the M23. It would take McLaren several years to catch up.**

Jody Scheckter flies past on the way to his stated goal of winning the world title in 1979. He had been signed as Ferrari's number one driver, with the less experienced Gilles Villeneuve as number two. But Villeneuve had won three races and Scheckter none as the championship reached round six in Belgium. Scheckter was given an ultimatum by the team: if he didn't win either of the next two races it would be obliged to shift the emphasis of its title campaign to Villeneuve. Scheckter being Scheckter, he won both races. His drive in Belgium was ragged, but it was a performance that perfectly illustrated the intensity of competitive desire that is essential to a top driver's make-up. At the end of the first lap his Ferrari 312T4 made contact with Clay Regazzoni's Williams, elbowing it aside to take sixth place. After then passing Mario Andretti's Lotus for fifth, Scheckter came upon the Brabham of Nelson Piquet and again made contact as he forced his way through. In his chase of Jacques Laffite's Ligier he then set the fastest lap of the race, despite near-full fuel tanks. As those remaining ahead of him hit problems, he cruised home to victory, his stature within the team now assured.

The Perfect Script

Cometh the age, cometh the man – and here he was in the hair trigger form of James Hunt: athletic build, cigarette in one hand, glamorous woman on the other – the antithesis of the cool, calculating professional.

By the mid-1970s the tobacco sponsors had all arrived and were basically funding F1. The more sophisticated money – car manufacturers, computer companies, banks – were not yet involved. There was, therefore, no carefully contrived image or profile and the personalities of drivers shone through. At the same time, TV was ensuring the sport had never had such a spotlight, had never been awash with such money. It created the perfect window of opportunity for celebrity-hood. Jackie Stewart, retired since the end of 1973, had assumed that role for F1 in the past, but his was an image of conformist, respectable glamour. The time was ripe for a rebel, someone who'd apparently walked into the sport directly from the world of rock-and-roll.

At the beginning of 1976 Hunt was newly signed by McLaren as a short-notice replacement for double world champion Emerson Fittipaldi. He had it all to prove – his way. He'd already told the team sponsor to forget the idea of him turning up at its functions in a blazer; if he came at all, it would be in his normal attire: barefoot, cut-off jeans, T-shirt, unkempt blonde hair. Now, as the final minutes

of qualifying for the season's first race ticked away, he was having a screaming row with his new boss, Teddy Mayer, about a modification he wanted on his car. Still seething, he snicked himself onto pole position, edging out Niki Lauda's Ferrari with a magnificent lap of raw aggression. The tone of the season had just been set, a season of see-sawing fortunes between these two men of diametrically opposed image.

If Hunt wasn't winning, he was crashing out, having altercations with marshals or with fellow drivers. Early in the season he was in the tabloids again when his wife left him for film legend Richard Burton. Then he was disqualified from a win for a technical infringement. Still this swirling mass of nervous competitive energy drove the McLaren like a man possessed, while Lauda, all calm and logic, glided his Ferrari from one immaculately prepared victory to another.

Driving racing cars scared Hunt. He made no bones about that. He was intelligent, had plenty of imagination and wasn't immersed in the same way of non-thinking as most of his peers. But he had a competitive drive that, with a whiff of victory in the air, could suppress that fear.

His team-mate Jochen Mass, a quiet, reflective fellow, could see clearly the neurosis in Hunt that drove his performances: "At a

The protagonists in the most remarkable narrative an F1 season has ever produced, Niki Lauda and James Hunt. This is the first half of 1976, before Lauda's scarring crash in Germany. Friends since their days on the junior slopes of the sport, they were thrown into the roles of foes on the track against a backdrop of conflict between their teams.

race he was intense, really highly strung, like a racehorse. On race morning he would quiver, totally oblivious to his surroundings, just totally gone. At one track he went to pee against a fence and did it facing the public stands instead of away, because he hadn't noticed. Everyone loves an eccentric driver, especially one who delivers – and he delivered. He was very, very demanding within the team and there was always a drama, a performance, about him and the team responded to it. My personality meant I found it very difficult to deal with."

Mayer: "James would often disappear round the back of the pits to throw up before a race. He got his performances from some place inside him and he seemed to need to get himself to this pitch to perform. As he became successful he became more confident and it made him believe that he could behave however he wanted to out of the car, as long as he was the star. It made him a wilder person, less conventional."

Hunt won two mid-season races in a row, but was again disqualified from one of them. Controversy stalked him. These disqualifications were invariably triggered by Ferrari – and here's another facet of the extraordinary story of that season: the political control of F1. The 'blazers' within the governing body had had their feathers ruffled by Bernie Ecclestone's increasing power over the last few years. McLaren was a leading light within (the renamed) FOCA, the powerful and largely British team association headed by

Ecclestone. Ferrari sat on the other side of the political fence with the old guard, the grandees, of the governing body. The Hunt disqualifications were seen very much in this light. "Yes, you could say there was a kind of paranoia in the paddock about the political side of it," says Mayer.

Just when the story could hardly get more dramatic, Lauda crashed at the German Grand Prix and suffered critical lung damage and facial burns. This was at the Nürburgring, the ultimate racetrack, opened in 1927 and host to Germany's premier race almost ever since. In an era of Stewart-inspired artificial venues, it was the last bastion of the matador age of F1. Lauda had been one of its most vociferous critics – even before his accident. Not only were its humps and switchbacks too severe for light modern constructions with significant downforce loadings on them, Lauda argued, but the track was too long to be marshalled properly. His crash proved him right on both counts. It was triggered by suspected suspension failure and he had to be rescued from his burning car by fellow drivers, not marshals. As he lay in hospital, Hunt won the race, just as he would have done in a B-movie script.

Lauda was administered the last rites in hospital, with doctors uncertain whether there was enough undamaged lung tissue to ensure survival. Within a few days it was clear that there was and his recovery after that was rapid. As they reduced his doses of

Hunt projected a rebellious, hard-living image that contrasted sharply with his rival Lauda's, even though they had much in common away from the tracks.

morphine, so things began to come back into focus. He held on to the one idea he knew was the key to his recovery: he was coming back as soon as possible to fight for his title. No way was he throwing it away. He'd had time to reflect on how he'd fought to get himself into this position: the gamble of borrowed money, the tricks of smoke and mirrors he'd used to get drives. Then the big chance: a drive with Ferrari for 1974. The *Scuderia* was coming off a poor season, but Lauda formed a close working relationship with its brilliant engineer, Mauro Forghieri – and worked. Work rate, applied logic and fight – that's what he was about. His relationship with Enzo Ferrari was feisty, but the old man didn't come to the races. So Lauda combined with Forghieri, utilising Mauro's genius while tempering his tangents with cool common sense. Lauda may have thought back to practice for the Spanish Grand Prix in his first championship year of 1975. After trying the car he reported back to Forghieri: "The car is understeering."

"No, it's not the car," retorted Forghieri. "You are driving on the wrong line of the track."

"Where?" asked Lauda.

"Oh, it's a corner around the back of the circuit."

"How do you know?"

"I have a friend watching there who tells me."

"Who's your friend?"

"Ah, it's the lady friend of my doctor."

"Fix my fucking understeer!"

Forghieri fixed the "fucking understeer" and Lauda qualified on pole position.

Lauda wanted more days like that. So rapid was his recovery he missed only two races, one of which was won by Hunt. Lauda's comeback was in Ferrari's backyard of Monza for the Italian Grand Prix. Yet more perfect scripting. Imagine the tension, the fever, as hundreds of thousands of rabidly enthusiastic Ferrari fans gathered to bear witness to a miracle at this Colosseum of speed, one of the world's fastest Grand Prix tracks.

With the burns to his skin still weeping blood onto his fireproof balaclava, Lauda returned to defend his championship 33 days after his accident, a month after those last rites. He qualified fastest of the three Ferraris. Three? Oh yes. Enzo had displayed his characteristic sensitivity to his drivers. He did not wish a scarred and almost certainly slowed Lauda to return, surely to lose to his healthier title rival and thereby besmirching the glorious image of Ferrari. Far better Lauda lose gloriously as the moral victor, out of sight, in his bed. As such, Ferrari had signed Carlos Reutemann – fast, enigmatic and handsome – to replace Lauda. But damn it, didn't the scarred, buck-toothed Austrian insist he was coming back! Ferrari could hardly publicly refuse him.

LEFT: **Niki Lauda makes his heroic return to F1 at Monza, just a month after being administered the last rites.**

FOLLOWING SPREAD: **James Hunt's McLaren M23 is tipped onto two wheels after colliding with Lauda's Ferrari 312T2 moments after the start of the 1976 British Grand Prix at Brands Hatch. Hunt's car was damaged and he took a short cut back to the pits to retire. The race was then red-flagged in order to clear the debris. The rules stated that any car that had retired in the first race was not allowed to take part in the restart, and Hunt was therefore out. When this was broadcast to the rabidly pro-Hunt crowd the scene turned ugly and there were genuine concerns about a riot starting. The organisers relented and allowed Hunt to restart. He caught and passed early leader Lauda and was first past the chequered flag – but was later disqualified.**

Lauda finished fourth, and for a time towards the end of the race was the fastest man on the track. "That was the most heroic performance I have ever witnessed in any sport," said no less a man than Stewart.

Hunt? Oh, the Italian officials ensured he was thrown to the back of the grid for an alleged fuel discrepancy and he crashed out while trying to make amends.

Three races to go, and Hunt needed to win at least two of them if he was to stand any chance of overhauling the big points cushion Lauda had built up earlier in the season. Impressively, he indeed won the next two Grands Prix to bring himself within three points of his rival as they headed for the finale in Japan. What more dramatic a backdrop to the story's conclusion than the brooding Mount Fuji?

Conditions on race day were appalling – heavy rain, thick mist – and there was talk of the drivers refusing to take part. Ecclestone applied a bit of pressure, and out they went.

Hunt took an early lead and was thereby the only man able to see where he was going. Back in the blinding spray, with his fire-damaged tear ducts not working properly, Lauda decided this was tantamount to suicide. He pulled in at the end of the second lap and withdrew from the fray.

Hunt needed now to finish third or better. He led for most of the distance but had to make a late, unplanned stop for new tyres, dropping him to fifth with just a handful of laps remaining. One of the cars he needed to pass was the Ferrari of Clay Regazzoni – Lauda's team-mate, a man with a reputation for being obstructive. But not this time; he was as good as gold, meekly pulling aside for the McLaren. Ah, here was another sub-plot. Regazzoni had given six years of loyal service to Ferrari and had been told by Enzo that he was safe for a seventh. Shortly before this race, however, he learned that this was not the case, that *Il Commendatore* had deceived him. He wasn't in the mood to help Ferrari's cause.

Hunt crossed the line third convinced he was fourth and that the title was lost – and that it was Mayer's fault for not bringing him in sooner to change tyres. So the season ended as it had begun, with Hunt screaming at his boss in the pits. Only this time Mayer was smiling and repeatedly holding up three fingers. Finally it dawned on Hunt: world champion, 1976.

Showbiz? There was an element of it, for sure. "There was a sort of pseudo-intensity about the season that has remained part of F1's make-up," says Mass. "It's not always really there, but you can create it by making everything more important than it really is. That's show business."

It was a magnificent story with a fascinating cast. It's a script that F1 has yet to better, and for the two heroes of the piece it was as real as real ever gets.

1971 – SLICK TYRES

Tyre performance had increased enormously throughout the 1960s as the cars developed stiffer chassis better able to utilise more grip, while the tyre companies' chemists responded with new constituents for better compounds and constructions. As the rubber worked more effectively so the trade-off between tyre grip and aerodynamic drag changed in favour of the former and tyres became ever-wider. The advent of wings and the downforce acting through the tyres increased their performance massively, but rather than going yet wider – with the associated cost in drag – the tyre companies sought to put more rubber on the road by making the gaps between the treads ever-smaller. By 1970 the treads were there only for heat dissipation. When new moulding techniques were developed to allow thinner coverings with less heat build-up, the need for the treads disappeared: the F1 slick was born (top left). Introduced by Goodyear, it appeared in the opening race of the season and won its first Grand Prix six weeks later, in Spain, fitted to Jackie Stewart's Tyrrell. Treaded tyres would be seen only in the wet from now on.

1977 – GROUND EFFECT

The Lotus 78 created downforce from its sidepods, utilising a phenomenon called ground effect. This downforce came with hardly any penalty in drag, the Holy Grail for any racing car designer. When a curved surface passes close to the ground at speed, the acceleration of the air between the curve and the ground reduces the air pressure and effectively sucks the body towards the ground. The necessary shapes were incorporated into the sidepods of the Lotus, sealed by skirts, giving the car a huge performance advantage.

Peter Wright, with encouragement and guidance from Colin Chapman, was the man at the centre of this development. The root of it, he says, were the wing failures on the Lotus 49s at the 1969 Spanish Grand Prix: "I was working for BRM then and [chief designer] Tony Rudd asked me whether it would be possible to get downforce without wings and we began looking at the idea in the wind tunnel. We started to build a wing-shaped car there, but it didn't have skirts and probably wouldn't have worked very well. The development of it was curtailed by the management."

Some years later Rudd and Wright were reunited at Lotus. Together with designer Ralph Bellamy, they built a wind tunnel model and noted that when the wing-shaped sidepods were sealed off with cardboard skirts, the downforce: drag ratio became vastly more efficient.

"We were a bit nervous about whether we would be allowed to run skirts as they might have been construed as a [banned] moveable aerodynamic device," explains Wright.

"We ran it with brush skirts originally and they didn't really work. Then we switched to polypropylene. But the real breakthrough came when we used ceramic tips to prevent the skirts wearing out. This allowed us to have a skirt that was sucked down by the pressure rather than sucked up against springs pressing downward. That transformed their efficiency."

The Lotus 79 of 1978 (top right) refined the principle with a layout that took fuller advantage. It was virtually unbeatable that year – except when Brabham came up with its short-lived 'fan car' (bottom left). Other teams copied Lotus's idea in their 1979 designs and two – Williams FW07 and Ligier JS11 – combined ground effect with super-stiff chassis able to fully translate the aero loadings to the tyres.

The performance gain was spectacular as maximum downforce increased from around 600kg pre-ground effect to around 2000kg – or four times the weight of the cars. The principle was best suited to engines with vee cylinder banks, which freed up the airflow behind the sidepods. This extended the life of the Cosworth DFV, and the independent teams that used it by helping them combat the turbos.

1977 – TURBOCHARGING

Forced induction via a mechanically driven supercharger had been all the rage in the Grand Prix racing of the 1920-30s and early post-war period. Basically, a turbine compresses the air, enabling more of it to be pumped through the engine, airflow being the primary limitation to horsepower. Using heat from the exhaust gases to drive the turbine – rather than a power-robbing mechanical drive – is the essence of turbocharging.

Forced induction became less feasible when in 1958 the F1 regulations were changed, specifying pump fuel rather than the cool-burning, alcohol-based fuels that had previously been allowed – and which were still permitted in America's Champcar single-seater championship.

Turbocharging soon became universal in the latter series, but in mid-1970s European racing its use was restricted to sports cars, where the equivalency formula was more favourable than F1's limit of 1.5 litres, half the permitted capacity of normally aspirated motors. This was deemed to be so severe a restriction that no one had bothered trying it since the formula came into force in 1966.

Renault's competition programme of the early 1970s was in sports car racing, where it ran a turbocharged car for the first time in 1975. François Castaing was the technical director of Renault Sport: "It was our sponsor Elf who first asked us what we would do if we went F1. They were very keen to take the turbo to F1, as the publicity of this new technology would be a terrific image-enhancer. The brains trust at Renault Sport was myself, Bernard Dudot and Jean-Pierre Boudy. Jean-Pierre was initially more convinced than me that a turbo was feasible for F1. We built an engine based on the sports car unit, but with just 1.5 litres. When we tested it on the dyno, straight away it had 500bhp, more than the normally aspirated engines of the time were giving – and we became very excited."

By 1976 it was being tested on the track.

"It all went well that winter," says Castaing. "But by the time we started racing it was the summer of 1977 and the increase in heat revealed to us the full misery of trying to race a turbo car on pump fuel. Our engine became famous for blowing up. In retrospect, I could have learned a lot if I'd read about the work done by the British companies when they were supercharging aircraft engines for the Second World War. We went through a very steep learning curve about combustions, how to control compressions and design pistons – all things that had already been well documented."

But those lessons were eventually learned, the turbo won its first race in 1979 (bottom right) and by '81 the Renault was racing with 600 horsepower – approximately 100 more than the opposition. By 1986, when the whole field was turbocharged, the fastest cars were qualifying with over 1400 horsepower. They remain the most powerful F1 cars ever.

War

Bernie Ecclestone made F1 so successful, brought in so much money, that there was a war – a territorial dispute between his band of brothers and a governing body re-energised by a new president. It lasted, on and off, for a couple of years in the early 1980s. It almost killed F1 – and the sport's greatest driver crashed to his death during it. Gilles Villeneuve perished following an accident at Zolder in final practice for the 1982 Belgian Grand Prix, a victim of circumstance, a convergence of factors almost all of which could be traced back to the sport's power struggle.

It really began in the mid-1970s when Ecclestone-era F1 was becoming so strong that car manufacturers began looking seriously at it. One of them, Renault, took the plunge. It did so with a radical turbocharged engine that within a couple of years was giving so much horsepower that the independent constructors, with their venerable Cosworth motors, could see a very clear long-term threat to their entire survival. If ever Renault achieved reliability, the specialists were going to get blown into the weeds and, well-funded though a lot of them were, they had nowhere near enough resource or knowledge – they were from the Cooper blueprint of bought-in engine technology, remember – to build and develop a turbo of their own. And if Renault started winning, other manufacturers would surely follow. Then where would the specialists be?

Fortuitously, the independents had stumbled upon an aerodynamic phenomenon called ground effect, and even more fortuitously it worked best in cars with an engine shaped exactly like the Cosworth DFV. That would buy the specialists a little bit of time;

with their superior understanding of single-seater dynamics, ground effect was a vital weapon against Renault and its turbo. But it would be only a matter of time before Renault, and any other manufacturer that followed it in, caught up.

At around the same time, FISA – the sporting arm of the FIA – for years weak and ineffectual, had got itself a new president: the bombastic, feisty Jean-Marie Balestre. He had vowed to take back control of F1 and place power properly in the hands of the body. An outrageously manipulative politician, he saw the emergence of the manufacturers – a strong power base separate from Ecclestone's FOCA group – as a golden opportunity. He viewed the differing interests of the two types of constructor as a fault line to be exposed and exploited.

While the FISA/FOCA war rumbled on, the turbos – with Ferrari now among their ranks – became more reliable and even faster; by the start of 1982 they had decent ground effect chassis of their own. Truly up against it now, the independents thought they saw a loophole in the regulations that allowed them to race up to 65kg lighter than the turbos; the governing body disagreed and disqualified them from first and second places in the Brazilian Grand Prix. In response, the FOCA teams announced they were not coming to Imola, the fourth round of the championship. It was a negotiating ploy that failed; Imola was run with just the non-FOCA teams, 14 cars instead of the usual 30-plus.

All of which left Renault and Ferrari, way quicker than the minor teams ranged against them, with an obligation to make the race look good, to prevent it becoming apparent that a championship

Gilles Villeneuve (far left) is mightily upset about Ferrari team-mate Didier Pironi's victory in the 1982 San Marino Grand Prix. To Villeneuve's left (in dark glasses) is the team's sporting director Marco Piccinini, who oversaw the pit instructions that day. Pironi had befriended Piccinini and Villeneuve suspected he had been duped. The anger this triggered was commonly believed to have been a contributory factor to Villeneuve's fatal accident during qualifying for the Belgian Grand Prix two weeks later.

without the FOCA teams would be a bad joke. It was put to the drivers – Alain Prost and René Arnoux at Renault, Villeneuve and Didier Pironi at Ferrari – that it would be helpful if they would co-operate in this aim. Arnoux recalls: "We agreed between the four of us that we would just put on a show for the first half of the race, that at half-distance we would make sure we were lined up in our grid order, and only then would we begin racing for real." We didn't know it then, but circumstances were playing a cruel trick on the Ferrari drivers and that that pre-race discussion at Imola was probably the defining click of fate.

Renault and Ferrari had the quickest cars of 1982, but only the Ferrari could combine its speed with reliability. A Ferrari driver was sure to be world champion, and Villeneuve seemed much the favourite of the two. Already acknowledged as the world's fastest driver, he'd comfortably outpaced Pironi in their year and a half together. But Pironi was wildly ambitious, a lethal team-mate to someone as proud and fearless as Villeneuve. Not that Gilles realised as much before this race. For him, Pironi was a friend as well as a team-mate. They had fun together, doing all the usual boys' stuff, and Gilles knew that when it came to speed in the car he had him covered – just as he had everyone else.

From a working class family in rural Canada, Villeneuve's had been an unlikely path to F1. A snowmobile champion in his homeland, he had transferred his uncanny balance to cars and become North American champion in a lesser category, Formula Atlantic. James Hunt – on the verge of securing the F1 world championship – had competed in a guest Atlantic race as

Villeneuve's team-mate and been comprehensively outperformed by him. He raved about this new talent to his McLaren F1 team, which ran an extra car for Gilles in the 1977 British Grand Prix. Straight out of a backwater championship, with no experience of F1 or the track, and in an obsolete car, Villeneuve had been set to finish fourth before a faulty temperature gauge intervened. Before the year was out he had been signed by Ferrari.

There were some wild moments among the phenomenal performances as he hurriedly learned his craft from a very low experience base, and for 1979 he accepted number two status to Jody Scheckter. But he expected payback for his loyal support to Scheckter's successful title campaign; he was to be given a clear run thereafter. Unfortunately, this came as Ferrari dropped the technical ball and it was all Villeneuve could do to produce occasional against-the-odds miracles in 1980 and '81. For 1982 Ferrari got its act together and the world's fastest driver was now just waiting for the rubber stamp of title authentication. But he had a team-mate of equal ambition, if not quite talent.

How could Pironi hope to combat such a phenomenon? Almost certainly recognising that he couldn't do it in the car, he worked at other ways. Patrick Tambay was a close friend of Villeneuve's and was later his replacement at Ferrari. He also knew Pironi very well. "Gilles just did his stuff," he says. "He didn't introduce into his reasoning that Didier might use tactics and strategy within the team. Gilles didn't play political games, whereas Didier… well, put it this way: Gilles didn't go for dinner or on holiday with the team's sporting director [Marco Piccinini], didn't

ask the sporting director to be godfather to one of his kids, didn't ask him to be best man at his wedding. I'm not being derogatory about Pironi, but that's how he operated." The wedding was the week before Imola; Villeneuve wasn't even invited – he put it down to an oversight.

At the beginning of the year, Pironi and Niki Lauda had led a drivers' strike; they were protesting FISA's imposition of new clauses on its Superlicence. It seemed just another piece of conflict in a sport that was suddenly full of it. But it also set Pironi in the role of negotiator between teams and drivers, a politician. Who better to broker an arrangement to put on a show at Imola between the drivers of two competing teams? The other three, all friendly with Pironi, readily agreed. For Pironi, such a ploy surely had a side benefit. He'd been outqualified by Villeneuve by 1.3 seconds but, at a stroke, his task of beating him had just been made half as difficult. Furthermore, the Ferraris were marginal on fuel consumption and might not have enough to go the distance. Both drivers understood the need not to run flat-out to the flag or, more critically, Pironi knew that Villeneuve understood this.

Prost's car failed early in the race but the others were good to their word and had the crowd on its feet with three-abreast moments and lots of lead changes. At half-distance they were lined up in qualifying order, as agreed: Arnoux, Villeneuve, Pironi. The racing began in earnest. Fifteen laps later Arnoux retired from the lead with a broken turbo, leaving Villeneuve and Pironi around half a lap clear of the field. Pironi continued to press Villeneuve hard; on the first lap following Arnoux's retirement both were under the lap

record. Concerned about their fuel consumption, the Ferrari pit prepared a sign saying 'Hold station'.

But during the ensuing lap Villeneuve took to the grass, allowing Pironi to overtake. So as they next passed the pits, with the sign now held out, Pironi was ahead. Each driver now had cause to believe they were the chosen 'winner': Villeneuve because he'd been ahead as the sign was prepared and because he'd been the quicker man all weekend; Pironi because he was in front when the sign was actually shown.

"Unfortunately, for personal reasons, I wasn't at the track that day," says Mauro Forghieri, the man who would normally have been in charge of Ferrari's team orders. "I would have given signals that were more specific. Gilles was an innocent believer. He had driven loyally to team orders in the past and suffered there when the car was not competitive. He was the faster driver and he was owed the result in Imola."

Villeneuve naively assumed Pironi was still just making a show of it, that he really intended to allow Villeneuve back in front. So each time Gilles got in front he would then back off, saving fuel. And each time Pironi would retake the lead. On the final lap Pironi outbraked Villeneuve at the last possible passing place, denying Gilles the chance to retaliate. Villeneuve was silently raging on the podium and vowed to others that all communication with Pironi was now over. So now we had a war within a war.

With 10 minutes to go in final qualifying at Zolder, and with Pironi having set the quicker time, Villeneuve went out on his final set of qualifying tyres and had a coming-together with a slower car

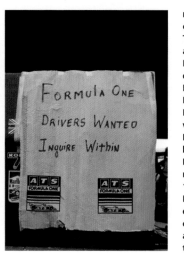

that sent his Ferrari airborne before nose-diving with extraordinary violence. Villeneuve was pronounced dead at 9pm.

The track was full of cruising non-turbo FOCA cars at the time Villeneuve had gone out, and it was with one of these that he collided. This practice had its roots in the FISA/FOCA war; FOCA cars would run underweight to set their qualifying time then be filled with ballast and sent out again. The use of 'sticky' one-lap qualifying tyres didn't help either; drivers were extremely loathe to back off lest they spoil their only chance of a fast time.

The last thing Villeneuve did – his last conscious act as a racing driver – as his car was launched was to switch off its engine to prevent the suddenly unloaded spinning wheels from over-revving it. A beautiful detail of a beautiful career that put into perspective the unsavoury tiffs of an immature sport. One of the first on the accident scene was Pironi. He was led away distraught.

"Gilles was in turmoil in the time between Imola and Zolder," says Tambay. "We spoke a lot on the phone at that time. He felt betrayed about what had happened there. He felt that what Pironi did to him there he had also been doing to him behind the scenes at Ferrari, and that he had just come to realise this. He was very, very upset. He'd put some pieces together in his head and come up with a picture he didn't like, one that shocked him perhaps more than it would have done had it been someone who truly understood Pironi better. That probably led to a misjudgement [from Villeneuve] in qualifying, an overreaction."

Ironically, with the sport's greatest driver now dead, a solution to the war started to become clear. During 1982 Ecclestone ran his

Brabhams with turbo engines from BMW. The turbo era was drawing other manufacturers in, just as the FOCA teams had feared, but most of them chose to do so without the pain of having to set up their own F1 design and manufacturing facilities and to instead be simply engine suppliers to established – FOCA – teams. With that critical competitive element resolved, negotiating the politics of a new peace was vastly simpler.

Zolder 1982 was a 'rivalry gone bad' sort of accident, triggered by the extremes of ambition and emotion the sport can generate. It was not in itself caused by the battle for control of F1, but the critical circumstances, the chances of fate that led to a death, were almost exclusively about that war. Furthermore, those destructive emotions flourish better in a malignant environment. The loss of F1's greatest exponent indicated to those outside the sport how far it had allowed politics and money to overshadow its essence.

This was a sport in a difficult stage of its evolution. Successful enough to be rich but not yet sophisticated enough to fully appreciate the picture it presented to the outside world. With battles ongoing, futures in the balance and a racing society still on familiar terms with driver fatalities, F1 barely even acknowledged Villeneuve's death – in stark contrast to the heart-rending outpourings 12 years later when Ayrton Senna died.

Even with an accord tentatively agreed, F1 still had a lot to do. It needed peace and stability between its government and its participants, and unless it was to resort to being a minority-interest 'matador' sport – with all the purity, blood and lack of corporate money that implied – it needed to make the sport still safer.

LEFT: The start of the 1980 South African Grand Prix – in the days before F1 developed a conscience about apartheid. The turbocharged Renaults of Jean-Pierre Jabouille (15) and René Arnoux are briefly overwhelmed by the snappier throttle response of the naturally aspirated Williams of Alan Jones, who has rocketed up from eighth on the grid. The turbos soon got into their stride, however, and Jabouille led from Arnoux by the end of this straight. It stayed that way until Jabouille retired with a punctured tyre, handing Arnoux the victory. Behind the Renaults are the blue Ligiers of Jacques Laffite (26) and Didier Pironi, and the neck-and-neck Williams and Brabham of Carlos Reutemann (28) and Nelson Piquet (5).

TOP RIGHT: Colin Chapman gets to throw his cap one last time. Elio de Angelis's Lotus 91 has just won the 1982 Austrian Grand Prix. At the end of the year Chapman died from a heart attack.

BOTTOM RIGHT: Gilles Villeneuve and Jody Scheckter were left to struggle through 1980 with the uncompetitive Ferrari 312T5. Villeneuve, freed from the constraint of being team number two, comprehensively outperformed Scheckter during the season.

FOLLOWING SPREAD:
Ayrton Senna, Alain Prost, Nigel Mansell and Nelson Piquet – probably the best drivers in the world at the time – line up in Portugal in 1986. With three races still to go, all were still in with a mathematical chance of the world title, though it was Prost who eventually won it.

LEFT: Keke Rosberg was Finland's first successful F1 driver. All balls and reflexes, he was a great improviser in the car. He won the world championship in 1982 and would later guide compatriot Mika Häkkinen to back-to-back world titles in 1998 and '99.

RIGHT: Nigel Mansell stomps away from his Williams FW10 after its Honda engine has blown in practice for the 1985 Canadian Grand Prix. The reach of the engine builders for ever-more horsepower was often beyond their grasp as the computer-controlled electronics were still fairly basic.

ABOVE: Gilles Villeneuve was the world's greatest driver at the time of his death during qualifying for the 1982 Belgian Grand Prix.

RIGHT: McLaren team-mates Niki Lauda and Alain Prost appear to be enjoying the view. They were locked in combat on the track over the 1984 world championship. Their McLaren MP4/2-TAG Porsches were by some margin the best

all-round package – speed/ reliability/fuel consumption – and so the only real competition they faced was each other. Prost was newly recruited to the team and Lauda soon discovered that he had no answer to the younger man's raw speed. He used instead the guile of experience and began each weekend with the aim of having the best possible car on race-day, even if that meant compromising

his qualifying performances. In the end a slightly better reliability record helped Lauda clinch the title – his third – by a scant half-point over Prost. It was no contest the following year: Prost dominated, while Lauda won only once, suffered an appalling reliability record and appeared to lack motivation. He retired – this time for good – at the end of the season.

LEFT: Ayrton Senna and Elio de Angelis shared an uneasy relationship as Lotus team-mates in 1985. De Angelis had been the number one for some time when Senna arrived. Team boss Peter Warr: "I offered Senna the number one position but he turned it down, said he just wanted equality. Elio realised pretty quickly that this guy was a bit special and to keep up with him was going to be bloody difficult. For the following year Ayrton said, 'Right, I want to be number one now', and I had to say to Elio, 'Look, we won't be needing you next year'. Elio's pride wouldn't have allowed him to stay there as number two."

TOP RIGHT: Senna celebrates victory in the 1988 Japanese Grand Prix – and his first world championship – after a majestic drive from 16th place at the end of the first lap.

BOTTOM RIGHT: The moment Nigel Mansell's 1986 world title disappeared. With 19 laps to go of the season's final race, his left-rear tyre exploded as he headed down Adelaide's Dequetteville Terrace at 190mph. Here he pulls off, having wrestled the car away from the walls while he brought the speed down. This incident obliged the Williams team to bring Nelson Piquet into the pits for a safety check– losing him the chance of the title, too. All of which left McLaren's Alain Prost to cruise home the winner of the race – and the championship.

LEFT: The grimy McLaren MP4/4-Honda of Ayrton Senna on its victory lap, Montreal 1988.

TOP RIGHT: Alain Prost talks to Senna before the Belgian Grand Prix of 1988, their first season together at McLaren. Theirs had always been a fractious relationship, but it was only after the Portuguese Grand Prix that 'war' was declared. As Prost had gone to pass Senna at the end of the first lap the Brazilian had edged him toward the pit wall at 180mph, forcing Prost so close that the signalling crews had to quickly pull up their boards. A furious Prost, who had gone on to win the race, later told his team-mate and title rival that if he wanted the championship so badly that he was prepared to die for it, he could have it. It was a perceptive comment, as it was this quality that did indeed separate the ruthless Senna from Prost.

BOTTOM RIGHT: Senna discusses a telemetry detail with McLaren designer Steve Nichols, while technical director Gordon Murray looks on. Nichols and Murray were responsible for the McLaren MP4/4 that won all but one race of the 1988 world championship.

FOLLOWING SPREAD:
The 1987 Portuguese Grand Prix is about to go green. Gerhard Berger's Ferrari F187 shares the Estoril front row with the Williams FW11B of Nigel Mansell, but it is the man third on the grid – Alain Prost in his McLaren MP4/3 – who is set to make history. Berger led for most of the distance, all fury and urgency, while Prost glided along in his wake before launching a stinging late-race attack on the Ferrari. Under increasing pressure and with his tyres losing grip, Berger spun with four laps to go, handing a victory to Prost that allowed him to overhaul Jackie Stewart's record of 27 Grand Prix wins. It was a classic Prost-style win: a glorious demonstration of finesse and brains.

Slaves to the Rhythm

Expansion by the designers, contraction by the lawmakers; that's been F1's yin and yang ever since the early 1980s. The designers claw yet more speed from thin air, only to have their wings clipped, keeping things safe and sane. Keeping F1 commercially on course. Keeping the money coming in.

Don't upset the apple cart, keep that gravy train rolling, another car manufacturer here, a computer giant there, TV audiences measured in billions. Keep the danger safe. Safety standards have improved beyond all recognition – more science in circuit design, better materials in the cars and a relentless will from the governing body.

As F1 had become better funded, so its cars got quicker faster. With imaginative design minds given the tools to feed their addiction, the fastest F1 car at the end of the 1960s was a full 26 per cent quicker than that of the beginning of the decade. Only in 1969, and with some encouragement from the drivers, did the governing body step in to restrict speeds, in this case via the limitation of wings. In general, they seemed content to let the boys play, even through the 1970s when the major safety advances came via alterations to circuits – more chicanes and guard rails, larger run-off areas – rather than the cars.

Only in the early 1980s, with the election of Jean-Marie Balestre as president of the sport's governing body, did ongoing performance restrictions become the norm. As he was also fighting a political battle for control of the sport with Bernie Ecclestone, Balestre's motives in limiting the recently applied ground effect technology were assumed to be for reasons other than safety. But history is kinder to him. There was little political capital to be made from the compulsory deformable structures and minimum-width pedal boxes he introduced in 1982. They were about driver protection – and this was just the beginning.

Performance was eventually controlled within very tight limits – the fastest car at the end of the 1990s was barely any quicker than that of the beginning, despite huge technology advances – and cars had to pass ever-more stringent crash tests.

The drive to make the cars faster occasionally provides a happy side effect of making them safer. This was so with the switch to carbon fibre rather than aluminium for monocoque construction in the early-to-mid 1980s. But it took legislation from the FIA to move the driver's feet behind the front axle line. In the 1960s one in every eight F1 accidents resulted in a fatality or a serious injury. This was down to one in every 250 by the early 1990s.

Speeds also needed to be contained to stop the human element from being overwhelmed. Without the banning of the technologies we'd now have cars with 3000 horsepower turbo engines and actively suspended, sliding-skirt ground effect chassis providing

Bernie Ecclestone's crowning glory as Brabham's owner came with Nelson Piquet's world title in 1983. Within three years Bernie had sold the team and was concentrating on running the sport.

FAR LEFT: Honda's turbocharged V6, as supplied to Williams in 1986. At 4 bar of turbo boost in race trim it produced 994bhp at 12,000rpm. In qualifying trim, at 4.5 bar, it gave 1150bhp. From just 1500cc.

LEFT: Nelson Piquet, on his slow-down lap having just won the 1986 German Grand Prix for Williams, gives McLaren driver Keke Rosberg a lift back to the pits. The latter had run out of fuel on the last lap, losing second place.

8g braking and 6g cornering – demands that would cause a driver to black out.

The turbo era brought the car manufacturer money in, but the sport's global marketing reach meant they stayed long after turbos were banned, supplying teams with cash and resource that designers and engineers had long only dreamed about. Wind tunnels were built, research and development programs initiated and the size of teams went exponential.

"When we won the championship in 1983," says designer Gordon Murray of his Brabham days, "there were about a dozen of us at the track and maybe another couple of dozen back at the factory." When Ferrari won its sixth world constructors' title in 2004, its aerodynamicists, software writers, mechanics, race engineers, logistics operatives, fabricators, research engineers, machinists, engine designers, transmission engineers, model makers, data analysts, departmental managers, composite specialists, truckies, wind tunnel engineers, designers, press officers, cooks and cleaners celebrated – all 800 of them.

The engineers may have had more money than ever to play with, but, paradoxically, ever-tighter regulations allowed them to do less with it than ever before. The environment of tight regulations and loose money has meant ever-smaller areas of advantage becoming ever-more significant, with hordes of clever people being unleashed on finding these tiny secrets. Stretching their competitively driven and imaginative minds, constantly being reined back every time they succeed, they weave forever more intricate webs. The governing body steps in and says, 'No!' The ground shakes, the engineers bitch – then scurry off to find new tiny secrets. And the cycle starts again. Laboratory speed rats, slaves to the desire to go faster.

Explained in this way the sport might look sillier than ever to the uninitiated outside world. But to the racing world it has its own logic, the same logic it's always had: faster, faster, use whatever's there. It's just that the environment has offered up juicier tools.

Like any change in F1 it has been of its time. Intricate searches within a microscopic area pose the ideal set of equations for computers to solve and IT typically accounts for over 50 per cent of a modern F1 team's staff. Yet nothing fundamental has changed – they are using microprocessors only to chase the same five fundamental performance parameters they've been chasing since 1968, finding forever more of the same through different routes, using different materials. So we've seen traction control, active ride, carbon fibre, electronic control of diffs and much more.

So how was it all controlled? How did the ragtag bunch of bandits and blazers of the FISA/FOCA war become the cohesive unit behind one of the most popular sports in the world?

Oh, it was beautifully subversive. The governing body was infiltrated, taken by stealth and with an eye on the long game. The governing body won the battle over Ecclestone and FOCA but made the mistake of thinking it had won the war.

Ecclestone's principal FOCA ally since the early 1970s had been Max Mosley, son of British fascist leader Sir Oswald Mosley and a man of rare intellect, someone who can entrance you with his charm even as he removes the very ground from beneath your feet. Since 1991 he has been president of the governing body, poacher turned gamekeeper – and Balestre, who had been FIA president since 1986, never saw it coming, knew nothing of the secret campaigning, the velvet whispers. FOCA is still headed by Ecclestone, South London second-hand car dealer made very good. It's good cop, bad cop, with each role interchangeable. And in this way Mosley and Ecclestone have delivered F1 to the promised land.

Their task was probably made simpler by the deaths of the only two figures with the force of personality to stand in their way, if they'd so chosen: Colin Chapman and Enzo Ferrari.

Chapman, founder of Lotus and the most creative F1 design mind of them all, died from a sudden heart attack in 1982. He'd already seen the way the technical wind was blowing, saw the diminution of the stage he was going to be allowed to work on. This became very clear to him when "they" banned his twin-chassis Lotus 88 of 1981.

This car was a conceptually brilliant way around the air separation that had previously been the limitation of downforce generated from the underbody, something that active ride was later able to achieve.

Peter Wright, the Chapman employee who thought of the twin-chassis concept, says: "It got around the rules. It was perfectly legal to the letter of the law, but it became pretty obvious there was no way it was ever going to be allowed to race. Chapman was extremely stubborn about it. He was fighting for the right to innovate. When the affair was all over he said to me, 'I've lost interest in racing. I'll keep going until the John Player [sponsorship] contract runs out'. He died, but I've a feeling he wouldn't have stayed around."

Lotus carried on for another 12 years but never really recovered from Chapman's passing. Ferrari might have gone the same way after Enzo died, aged 90, in 1988. But Ferrari, unlike Lotus, was supported by deep, deep pockets. It flailed for some years, but eventually a man with a vision, Luca di Montezemolo, rescued it and built the foundations for the colossus of a team it has since become, stronger than ever it was in Enzo's day. Besides, F1 without Ferrari? That would have been very bad for business.

One day quite recently, when he was already past normal retirement age, Bernie looked at what he'd created and tried to work out how to get the hell out. Here indeed was a problem to be reckoned with.

TOP LEFT: **Goodyears in Detroit, 1985.** These were the dominant F1 tyres of the time, given a clear run once Michelin had withdrawn at short notice at the end of 1984.

BOTTOM LEFT: **Piercarlo Ghinzani's Ligier JS29B makes a fiery exit from the 1987 German Grand Prix,** its previous-generation Megatron turbo engine well ablaze, forced beyond its limits by the sport's competitive drive.

RIGHT: **Mario Andretti's last full season of F1, 1981 with Alfa Romeo, did not go well. His dissatisfaction shows as Alfa's racing boss Carlo Chiti talks.** Like most things of the time the root of the problem was the ongoing row between the teams and the governing body over regulations. "It was so frustrating," says Andretti. "I could not get through to Chiti. I had some horrendous fights with him. I never before heard of a driver having to fight with his engineer just to try some different springs. This was at the time when everyone was using the ride height 'cheat' to get around the regulations limiting ground effect. But Alfa, even though everyone else was doing it, refused to do it. Chiti would have the car sprung so stiff it wouldn't come down and give us the downforce we needed by sealing the underbody to the track. Gianni Morelli was my engineer, a good guy, but even he was totally ineffective with Chiti. I mean, Chiti would literally bop him on the head to settle any arguments! I used to say to Gianni, 'Now, okay, you might get whacked, but go over there and tell him this is what we want to do'. It's funny now – but it was just frustrating at the time."

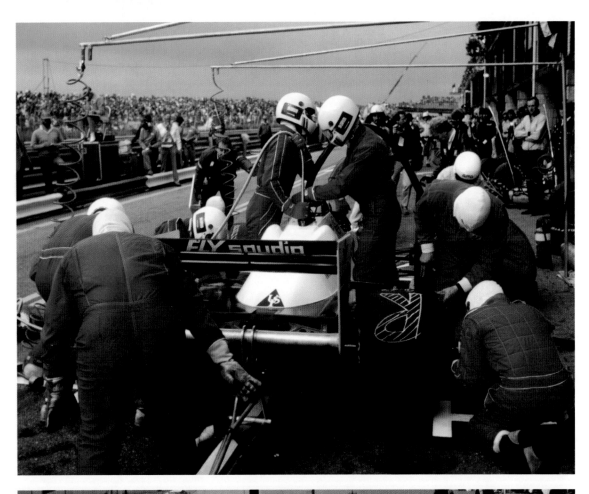

TOP LEFT: **Mid-race refuelling – a race strategy reintroduced to F1 in 1982, after a gap of 25 years, by Brabham's Gordon Murray – had caught on fully by mid-1983. Keke Rosberg stops his Williams FW08C for fuel during the Dutch Grand Prix.**

BOTTOM LEFT: **A time of transition, Detroit 1984. Specialist constructor Williams entered a partnership with manufacturer Honda who supplied the team its turbo V6 engine. The ban on refuelling for 1984 is reflected in the huge fuel tank between cockpit and engine on these Williams FW09s. At the time of a widespread move to carbon fibre construction, these cars were the last from any frontline F1 team to be fashioned from aluminium.**

RIGHT: **In an era where conflict seemed to be everywhere, Carlos Reutemann – seen here in the 1980 Canadian Grand Prix – played his part by bringing it to Williams when he disobeyed team orders to beat Alan Jones in the 1981 Brazilian Grand Prix. The two drivers ceased communication forthwith. After the final race of the season – after he had just lost the world championship following a puzzlingly low-key performance – Reutemann approached Jones to suggest they bury the hatchet. The candid Australian replied: "Yeah, in your back, mate!"**

LEFT: The turbocharged Renault V6 1.5-litre turbo that changed the complexion of the sport, the engine that dared accept the regulation penalty of half the capacity of a non-turbo F1 motor. It was an engine that began life with no F1 aspirations, as a non-turbo 2-litre unit for sports car racing in 1972, designed by Jean-Pierre Boudy and François Castaing. The latter recalls: "It had a cast-iron block because we wanted to ensure it was very rigid and not as affected by temperature variation as an aluminium block. We wanted this because we were trying to minimise the amount of oil and needed to ensure good oil flow to the bearings. The thinking behind minimising the oil was very much of the time; it was believed an engine would succeed or fail not so much on combustion efficiency but on scavenging the oil properly and ensuring that oil in the crankcase could flow properly and not build up due to pressure cycles. Anyway, quite by chance, that engine was very suitable for turbocharging because of this strong block."

Castaing and Boudy worked for Renault offshoot Gordini. There was another Renault splinter company, Alpine, for which the engineer Bernard Dudot worked. Dudot was fascinated by the idea of turbocharging and had been trying the concept in rallying. The two companies were merged to form Renault Sport in 1973, with Castaing in overall charge. Under Dudot's influence, the sports car engine was turbocharged from 1975 and met with some success. Both the parent company and team sponsor Elf then began asking the Renault Sport engineers about the feasibility of F1, attracted by the increasing marketing reach of the sport under Bernie Ecclestone's management. A 1.5-litre version of the 2-litre sports car unit was the engineers' answer and soon an F1 prototype was testing. "At first we were very far away from competitive F1 times," says Dudot, "and we had terrible turbo lag. The problems with the engine were mainly detonation and piston-related. This meant that when they failed there was lots

of smoke, very spectacular, and everyone soon knew about it."

The Renault RS01, F1's first turbocharged car, made its debut at the 1977 British Grand Prix. In twin-turbo guise the engine won for the first time in France two years later. The political as well as technical ramifications to the sport were enormous.

TOP RIGHT: René Arnoux's turbocharged Ferrari 126C3 makes a fuel stop during the 1983 German Grand Prix. He went on to dominate the race. Arnoux had been catapulted into the big time by Renault but had parted company from the team at the end of 1982 after causing a rift by refusing to pull aside for team-mate Alain Prost in the French Grand Prix, having initially agreed to do so. At Ferrari he fought for the 1983 world championship with Prost and Renault, though ultimately both men lost out to Nelson Piquet's Brabham. Arnoux never scaled such heights again and by his final season, 1989, was a shadow of the raggedly aggressive driver whose style had meshed so well with the super-powerful turbo cars.

BOTTOM RIGHT: The turbocharged Renault gave its mechanics plenty to do for the first few years of the team's F1 participation. Its reliability was much better by 1984.

LEFT: Despite the sport being split asunder by rows over money, the commercial freight train kept right on running. The Giacobazzi girls looked bored with it all at Imola in 1981.

RIGHT: Prof Sid Watkins, F1's permanent doctor, gets in on a glamour photo shoot. His racing involvement began when he served as chief doctor at Watkins Glen from 1962 while working in America. When he returned to his native UK in 1970, he did a similar job at Brands Hatch and came to know Bernie Ecclestone, who eight years later recruited him to upgrade the medical care for all Grands Prix. Watkins oversaw a revolution in F1 medical standards before standing down at the end of 2004.

FOLLOWING SPREAD:
LEFT: The enigmatic Carlos Reutemann, with the world championship finally within his grasp, lets it all slip away at the eleventh hour at Las Vegas in 1981. By the halfway point in the season he had built up a comfortable lead in the championship thanks to some brilliant performances in his Williams FW07C. But even at that point he felt doomed and placed a bet against himself with a journalist. Going into the final round he was one point ahead of Brabham's Nelson Piquet. He secured pole position with a stunning lap but was only fifth into the first corner and, unnerved by a mismatched set of tyres, fell further back until Piquet passed him relatively easily. He eventually faded to finish out of the points, while Piquet – semi-conscious through heat exhaustion – struggled home fifth, enough to snatch the title from under Reutemann's nose.

RIGHT: Didier Pironi's turbocharged Ferrari engine blows during practice for the 1981 Monaco Grand Prix. The year before, driving for Ligier, he had set pole position at the track. This time, in the poor-handling Ferrari 126CK, and denied running time by this engine failure, he was only 17th-fastest. Yet his team-mate Gilles Villeneuve qualified an identical car a superb second, 2.5 seconds faster. In the race Pironi did well to finish fourth. But he was lapped by the winner: Villeneuve.

1981 – CARBON FIBRE CONSTRUCTION

Ground effect demanded cars with the maximum possible sidepod venturi area within the maximum width allowed by F1's regulations. But conversely they also demanded super-stiff chassis to properly convert the aerodynamic loads to the tyres. A problem: the wider the venturis, the narrower the cockpit, the weaker the structure. A new material was needed. Aluminium had been the designer's choice for decades and aluminium honeycomb had enabled them to make stiffer structures since the mid-1970s. But now it had reached its limit.

John Barnard was a young designer working on a Marlboro-funded F1 project for aspiring team owner Ron Dennis. He had been thinking in terms of steel, pondering that the cost in weight might be overcome by the benefits in stiffness. He was then introduced to aerospace composites manufacturer Hercules, who produced for him an F1 chassis in carbon fibre (top left). Sheets of this material were laid out in the form required, impregnated with resin and baked in an autoclave. For the same weight as an aluminium chassis – around 35kg – it was twice as stiff. The resultant car, the McLaren MP4/1, was able to enjoy the aerodynamic benefits of significantly bigger ground effect-generating venturis than the competition, without compromising chassis stiffness.

1982 – TELEMETRY & ELECTRONIC CONTROL

Preventing the highly stressed turbocharged engines from blowing themselves to pieces required intricate control of their fuelling and ignition – more intricate than the prevailing mechanical systems could provide. Bosch then introduced the electronic control unit (ECU) in the BMW F1 turbo engine fitted to the Brabhams (top right). Concurrently, in order to monitor what was happening inside the engine, to give the engineers a chance to tell the driver to switch off before it blew, it also pioneered transfer of information by radio wave: telemetry.

Brabham designer Gordon Murray recalls: 'The first ECU they gave us was the size of a biscuit tin. Getting it to work properly was a nightmare. We tested one day at Donington Park and couldn't get the thing to run properly. Then the guy from Bosch came up with a programme that worked and the driver came in and said, 'It's magic – driveable and quick.' They

took the box back to Germany, plugged it into the wrong voltage and burned it out. That cost us 12 months of development.

"The turbo engines were pretty undriveable in the early days: a little four-cylinder 1.5-litre with a huge truck turbo running several bar of boost. Add in early electronic control and it was like sitting on an Exocet missile with no control system. But they progressed to the point where we were able to win the world title in 1983."

1982 – REINTRODUCTION OF PIT STOPS

After a gap of 25 years, Murray reintroduced the planned tactical pit stop to F1 (bottom left): "That was purely a mathematical thought. I was working out how much each extra kilo of weight cost you per lap on the average circuit. But I could never work out why in the first part of the race – from full to half-tanks – there wasn't quite the same advantage as from half-tanks to empty. And, of course, it's obvious: it's the height of the centre of gravity of the car, not just the weight. We had a single tank, so the height of the fuel when full was pretty high. So I did some sums.

"If you start on half-tanks you get the advantage of half the fuel load *and* a lower c of g. I then worked out the time penalty of slowing down, refuelling and accelerating for a pit stop and realised that it was less than the time saved in lap times. For the purposes of the comparison I ignored the fact that you'd be on new tyres and that you could use tyres of a softer, grippier compound because they didn't have to last as long. That was just the icing on the cake.

"We were looking for something like a 30-second stop to ensure it was quicker than not stopping. We booked a circuit for a day to practice pit stops in secret and we got it down to 26 seconds – quick for those days, but crap today."

Hand in hand with this development was the popularisation of radio communication from pits to driver and vice versa in order to co-ordinate the stops.

1983 – GROUND EFFECT CURTAILED

The governing body tried several times in the early 1980s to limit ground effect, arguing that the speed increase it generated was making the circuits obsolete. In 1981 a minimum ride height of 6cm was imposed, but the teams got around it with hydraulic suspensions that allowed the cars to run close to the ground on the track but

which were at the regulation minimum when inspected in the pits. These driver-actuated ride heights were banned, along with sliding skirts, for 1982. This led the teams to run virtually solid suspensions to keep the low ride heights – necessary for ground effect – constant.

Ground effect was successfully curtailed by a rule stipulating that the whole underside of the car within a specified area had to be completely flat, while skirts of any sort were banned. This meant no ground effect-inducing venturi shapes.

The area behind the rear axle line was not covered by this regulation and so teams took to building a venturi shape there: a diffuser. But initially it was nowhere near as effective as the old sidepod venturis because of limited airflow area and a lack of skirts.

1984-88 – TURBOS STRANGLED

As part of an exercise in speed containment, the governing body phased out turbocharged engines with increasingly stringent limitations before finally implementing an outright ban. From 1984 a maximum of 220 litres of fuel was imposed and fuel stops were banned, which meant the turbo cars had to reduce their boost pressures so as not to run out of fuel. In 1986 this limit was further reduced to 195 litres. In 1987 maximum boost was restricted to 4 bar by the use of a pop-off valve; normally-aspirated cars of 3.5 litres were now allowed and they could run with a 40kg lower weight limit and no fuel maximum. The following year turbos were restricted to 2.5 bar and a fuel allowance of 150 litres. All this brought down maximum horsepower to approximately 650bhp in race trim, compared to around 920bhp in 1986.

1989 – NEW FORMULA

MAXIMUM ENGINE CAPACITY: 3.5 litres normally aspirated. Turbos banned.

1989 – SEMI-AUTOMATIC GEARCHANGE

The Ferrari 640, designed by John Barnard, introduced an electro-hydraulic gearshift operated by 'paddles' on the steering wheel (bottom right), with automatic actuation of the clutch. Its shifts were quicker, the driver could have both hands on the wheel at all times, and because a gear lever was no longer required, the cockpit could be narrower, thus reducing drag

Spiritual Thuggery

With the sport's very nature changing around them, the drivers barely noticed – foot down, bank balance up, as they benefited from the great safety strides made on the backs of surrendered past lives.

But then came an extraordinary man: Ayrton Senna. The Darwinian evolution of the racing driver mutated here. The top men had always maximised all areas that contained a competitive advantage – except the base instinct to commit deliberate fouls. In the past this had been tempered by the consequences. Dan Gurney, Grand Prix star of the 1960s, said: "It wasn't that that sort of thing didn't cross your mind, but given the cars and the circuits we raced them on, you just felt honour bound not to do it."

Alain Prost was the last F1 standard-bearer who raced to the 'Gurney' rules. Senna – who didn't so much have the baton handed to him as physically intimidate Prost into giving it to him – was the first to act on the implications of the safety margins now built into the cars and tracks. He felt he drew upon deeply spiritual places to produce some of the mesmerising performances he was capable of. But when push came to a little mid-corner brake test, he was very definitely of this world. And maybe Prost was right when he said that Senna believed God would always protect him. Whatever, it meant Prost felt he had no answer to the resultant spiritual thuggery of this most complex of men and the intense rivalries that are part of any motor racing age took on a harder, more cynical edge.

Senna's clinching of the 1990 world championship by the simple expedient of deliberately driving into Prost at the start of the Japanese Grand Prix was the most infamous piece of such behaviour from this charismatic, paradoxical man. It came 12 months after he'd lost the title to Prost after a similar, but much tamer collision caused by Prost.

"We all have weaknesses," says Senna's then-boss Ron Dennis. "I think Ayrton might well have read the section in his own particular guidebook that said an eye for an eye, a tooth for a tooth. I wasn't supporting it but I enjoyed the benefit of it, so you find yourself torn. But in the conversation that took place – not at that moment, but much later – I don't think he was proud of that particular judgement. It was not one of his finest moments, and in the end even he could not justify it."

But still there was the artistry to admire, still the same fascinating improvisation of technique to study. In the early 1990s traction control came to F1 drivers' aid. This was a very emotionally

Ayrton Senna doing what he did 41 times in F1: spraying the victory champagne. Spiritual, emotional and warm, in the car he had a ruthless streak. He used emotion to boost his performances, enabling him to dig deeper into his reserves than any other driver before or since and produce some otherworldly results. But the same emotion led to unreasonable on-track behaviour, to the point where his great rival Alain Prost felt unable to reach mutually acceptable terms of combat.

FAR LEFT: Ayrton Senna walks away from his controversial collision with Alain Prost at the start of the 1990 Japanese Grand Prix.

LEFT: Senna talks to his good friend Prof Sid Watkins at the 1990 Spanish Grand Prix. They would talk frankly on the day before Senna's death, the day that one of his peers, Roland Ratzenberger, had been killed during qualifying for the 1994 San Marino Grand Prix. Watkins advised that, given his emotional turmoil, the time was right for Ayrton to walk away from the sport. "No, I cannot give this up," Senna replied.

difficult moment for enthusiasts, but still Senna and Prost were demonstrably the best out there. And the reasons for that underline how participant reality and onlooker perception can vary wildly. Whenever grip overwhelms power, which it had done on and off n F1 for decades, the critical part of the turn is the entry, not the exit where traction control did its supposedly evil work. Taking the absolute maximum possible speed into the corner, transferring on-the-limit braking force into on-the-limit cornering force, has been the key to being quick in F1 for a long time. Prost and Senna were masters at it – but achieved it in very different ways.

Prost would turn into a corner earlier (and more gently) than dictated by the geometric ideal – the shortest distance between two points. Turning from a shallower angle, he could maintain speed for longer. Ordinarily that would then leave him with the problem of arriving at the apex at the wrong angle – with not enough axis-change in the car's direction. But he would overcome that by how carefully he shifted the weight distribution under braking and by setting the car up to have a grippy front end that would support him subtly pivoting the whole car around its outer front tyre. It looked undramatic but could be devastatingly quick, especially when he was able to tune the car's set-up to the pinnacle of perfection.

Senna didn't worry as much about perfecting the set-up, preferring to use improvisation in the cockpit to make up for that last little bit of car deficiency. His technique was centred around more conventional lines than Prost's, with a later turn-in much closer to the geometrical ideal. He'd save time by getting axis-change into the car early, too, but from where he turned there was less time to do this. Which was where his distinctive throttle-jabbing came into play. His Honda race engineer Takeo Kiuchi explains: "Drivers normally try to be as smooth as possible in this phase, and their corner entry, determined by the tyre grip, determines their speed all the way through the corner. But with Ayrton, always he was on and off the throttle very fast. And each throttle application was perfectly timed to use the engine torque to change the yaw of the car a little bit at a time so that the tyre didn't give up and give him a big slide. Other drivers tried it, but only Ayrton could make it work."

At the end of 1993 Prost retired and Senna left McLaren, his home of six years, to replace Prost at Williams for the promise of a straightforward fourth title, perhaps paving the way for a life away from the raw edge he'd always inhabited. But then things got Wagnerian. What was in that blue Benetton? Aside, that is,

OPPOSITE: Senna in extremis. Still carrying a grudge for how the title had been decided between them the year before – when Prost had clumsily driven into Senna at Suzuka rather than be bullied out of the way, and the FIA had disqualified Senna for missing out a stretch of track as he recovered from the incident – Senna decided the 1990 championship in his own favour by deliberately driving his McLaren into the back of Prost's Ferrari in Japan. It was a cynical move, committed in the full knowledge that if neither of them finished Prost would not be able to overhaul Senna's points lead in the one remaining race.

from a driver, Michael Schumacher, with a gift on a par with Senna's and the hunger of having it all to do. The electronic gizmos, traction control and such, had been banned for 1994, but Senna noted with dismay that Schumacher's car behaved as if the changes hadn't happened. Suddenly, far from stepping back from the brink and having an easy ride, Senna was having to dig deeper into those spiritual reserves than ever before.

Pride was at stake, apart from everything else, as Schumacher shadowed Senna's every move – once the safety car had been called in – during the early stages of the San Marino Grand Prix. Senna raised his game to near-impossible levels to keep the slower car ahead; Schumacher was content in the knowledge there was no way Ayrton could keep that up for 60 laps and that all he had to do was keep pushing him. "It was tragic," says John Watson, F1 star of a previous generation. "It was the law of the jungle playing out right in front of your eyes, the young lion pushing and prodding, looking to take his place at the head of the pride. It was going to be cruel whichever way it happened."

Through a flat-out kink something goes wrong and Senna is heading off the track towards a retaining wall. Only the day before, in practice, Roland Ratzenberger had become F1's first race meeting fatality for 12 years, shattering the illusion that the sport was now safe. So as Senna hits the wall at an angle, still travelling at more than 130mph, it can no longer be assumed he'll be okay.

He dies.

F1, lulled by over a decade of death-free races, went into deep shock, took a long, hard look at itself and addressed the issues. The audiences continued to grow, the money still swept in and Schumacher came to dominate like no driver had ever done before, frequently using the sort of questionable tactics popularised by Senna. Back in 1980, when Schumacher was still a kid racing go-karts, he'd watched Senna – then at the end of his karting career – and had been taken aback at how he could do things differently to any other driver he'd ever seen. Now, when yet another record falls to him and the remarkable talents of those he has gathered around him at Ferrari, Michael will occasionally be asked about Senna and you can't help but feel for him as he struggles not to let his emotion show. For all the money, marketing and TV audiences, don't let anyone tell you there isn't still a gladiatorial essence to this sport.

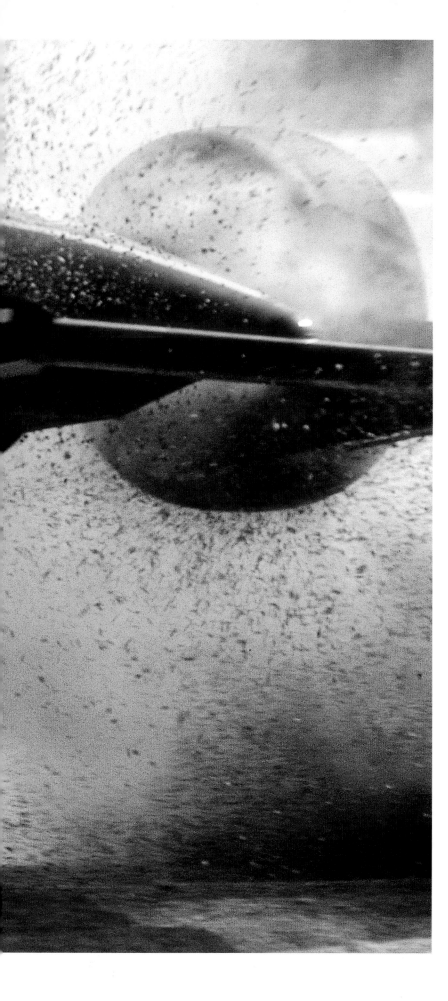

Aguri Suzuki launches his Lola 90-Lamborghini over the kerbs during practice for the 1990 Italian Grand Prix at Monza; he would finish sixth in the race. Later that season he would score the first podium finish for a Japanese F1 driver, finishing third in his home Grand Prix.

LEFT: Ayrton Senna and Michael Schumacher, the King and the Pretender, on race morning at Imola in 1994. Later in the day they were in this position on the track– Senna pushing, Schumacher prodding – when Senna crashed to his death at Tamburello.

TOP RIGHT: Nigel Mansell scrutinises the timing screens with Williams's technical director Patrick Head and engineer David Brown.

BOTTOM RIGHT: Schumacher's quest for the 1999 world championship ended with this leg-breaking accident on the first lap of the British Grand Prix. Attempting to recover from a poor start, he went to pass team-mate Eddie Irvine in the 190mph braking zone for Stowe Corner. But a hydraulic leak to the rear brakes meant he had front braking only and his Ferrari F399 skated off the track, hitting the tyre barriers at 66mph. His right leg was fractured in two places and he missed the next six races.

ABOVE: Another title-deciding professional foul, this time from Michael Schumacher at Adelaide in 1994. After crippling his Benetton's front suspension through sliding into a barrier, his only hope of securing the title was to take out the Williams of rival Damon Hill. As Hill dived for the inside, Schumacher turned in on him, tipping the Benetton onto its side. Damon's suspension was also terminally damaged now and so Michael won the title by a single point.

RIGHT: Nigel Mansell, on his victory lap at the 1991 British Grand Prix, gives Ayrton Senna – whose McLaren had run out of fuel – a lift back to the pits. But even at this moment Senna was still competing: what Mansell didn't know was that Senna was memorising the readouts on the Williams's dashboard so that he could immediately report them to Honda, his engine supplier, in case there was any useful information that could be used to his future advantage.

FAR LEFT: Michael Schumacher: seven world titles and – on the eve of the 2005 season – 83 Grand Prix victories.

LEFT: Ayrton Senna: three world titles and 41 Grand Prix victories. He would surely have won more…

ABOVE: Martin Brundle's Jordan 196-Peugeot inverts itself at Turn Three in Melbourne, the opening seconds of the 1996 season. The impact was huge, but Brundle, who was in his last season of F1, rushed back to the pits, was given the okay by medics and jumped into the team's spare car. He took the restart from the pit lane and retired after a collision with the Ligier of Pedro Diniz on the first lap. He later admitted that he had forgotten his car had cold brakes; it had not been allowed to tackle the aptly named warm-up lap.

While refuelling stops were banned – from 1984 to '93 – cars had to carry around 180kg of fuel at the start of races. This caused them to bottom-out over bumps and so teams had to fit skidplates to stop the chassis being damaged. In the interest of lightness these were made from titanium, the side benefit of which were impressive 'fireworks displays'.

ABOVE: Mika Häkkinen launches his McLaren MP4/8-Ford over the Adelaide kerbs during practice for the 1993 Australian Grand Prix. Having served most of the year as McLaren's test driver, Häkkinen was bursting to prove his speed when he was given three races by the team at the end of the season, replacing the disappointing Michael Andretti. In the first of these outings, at Estoril in Portugal, he outqualified his legendary team-mate Ayrton Senna. "It was funny," says Jo Ramirez, former McLaren team co-ordinator. "Mika was smiling away after qualifying and Ayrton was irritated by this. 'How many races have you won?' he asked Mika. 'How many championships, eh?' But this just made Mika smile even more. Senna overtook the upstart on the first lap of the race – in a very uncompromising manner. Mika qualified fifth on this particular occasion.

RIGHT: Michael Schumacher – here going off in practice at Spa in 1996 – has been criticised for having more such accidents than previous great champions. But this criticism is not comparing like with like. Schumacher has competed in an era where safety standards mean the penalty for these incidents is usually not that great. He has used this to establish absolute limits in a way that would not have been feasible in more perilous eras.

FOLLOWING SPREAD:
LEFT: Ayrton Senna and his McLaren MP4/8-Ford in the process of winning the 1993 Monaco Grand Prix, his sixth victory in F1's most glamorous race. Perhaps significantly, he inherited this win after Schumacher retired his similarly powered Benetton B193 from a commanding lead because of a fire caused by a leak of hydraulic fluid.

RIGHT: Senna celebrates his 50th F1 pole. There were another 15 to come before his death in 1994 – the only record of his that Schumacher hadn't beaten by the end of 2004.

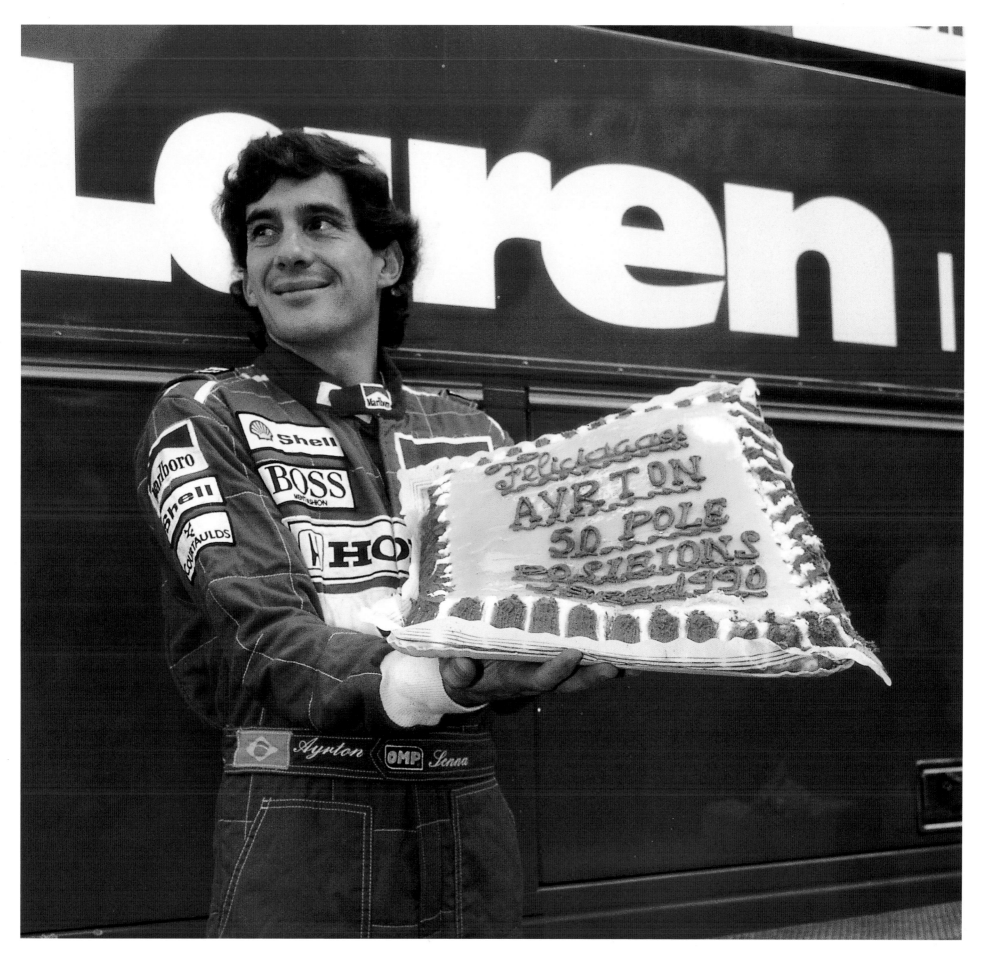

Nigel Mansell had a fanatical following at the height of his success in the early 1990s, by which time Mansellmania had spread as far as Japan (right). His Italian fan base grew enormously when he joined Ferrari for 1989 (left). During the following two seasons his swashbuckling driving led him to be labelled by the *tifosi* as *Il Leone* – 'The Lion'. A hugely complex character, Mansell had a difficult F1 apprenticeship, and it took a long time to unlock his potential. But he was used to toughing it out. As a struggling F3 driver he got the chance of a lifetime when he was invited to test for the Lotus F1 team in 1980. He accepted, without revealing he had a broken bone in his neck following a crash at Oulton Park. Colin Chapman, who came to look upon Mansell as his protégé, promoted him to a full-time race seat in 1981. Chapman's death from a heart attack at the end of 1982 was a big blow to Mansell's prospects. But his career received a lifeline when Frank Williams signed him for 1985. In a less hostile environment, Mansell began to flower and took his first Grand Prix victory at Brands Hatch in 1985 – immediately following it with another in South Africa. He narrowly lost the 1986 world title, and put himself out of a title challenge in the penultimate race of the following season with a practice crash that injured his back.

Emboldened by success during this time he had become a hugely exciting performer, daring to make outrageous passing moves that most would shy away from. He was a total showman and would never do it the easy way; the hard way always looked more dramatic. But it was easy to see why the Ferrari fans took him to their hearts, especially after he won on his debut for the team in Brazil. He fell out with Ferrari in 1990 after Alain Prost joined, feeling slighted that the reigning champion had changed the team's focus.

Mansell rejoined Williams for 1991 at just the time its partnership with Renault and the work of aerodynamicist Adrian Newey were maturing. With the Williams FW14B-Renault of 1992 he enjoyed a massive machinery advantage and dominated the world championship. His and Frank Williams's view of his financial worth were at a variance, though, and he left F1 as reigning champion, transferring to the American CART series, which he won at his first attempt. He returned to Williams as an occasional stand-in during 1994 in the wake of Ayrton Senna's death and triumphed in the final race of the year, Australia, aged 41. A planned full comeback with McLaren in 1995 stalled early after the car proved uncompetitive.

Thierry Boutsen charges through the kink in the Monaco tunnel in the 1989 Williams FW12C-Renault. He was in third place when forced to make an early pit stop because of a delaminating rear wing. Such is the downforce generated by F1 cars at these speeds, they could, in theory, run along this tunnel's roof.

Schuey Versus Newey

The King and the Pretender walked into the auditorium for the third joust of their 1994 spat and only one of them walked out. The Pretender had become King.

After the shock and grief had subsided, F1 realised that its underlying weakness had been exposed: Michael Schumacher was left without a true rival. The only way any of his peers could compete with him was to be behind the wheel of a faster car. So Schumacher's 'apparent' rivals came and went. But what they had in common was they drove cars designed by master aerodynamicist Adrian Newey. For six years after Ayrton Senna's death, F1 distilled into a battle between Schuey and Newey. It wasn't sold like that, but that's how it was.

Senna versus Schumacher in comparable machinery would have been an enthralling contest, one that F1 could have thrived on for years, one that would've needed no explaining, no caveats. But that dream died at Tamburello on May 1, 1994. In the commercial age, the sport had sold itself on conflict between individual gladiators – Hunt vs Lauda, Piquet vs Jones, Prost vs Lauda, Mansell vs Piquet, Prost vs Senna – but really those contests had only been covering up an inconvenient truth about the nature of the sport: it's so machinery-dependent that it struggles to tell us anything definitive about the human merit behind a driver's race victory.

Actually, the sport had always been like this. But the sport had not always previously made such vast sums of money selling itself to general TV audiences who were attracted by personalities and the clashes between them rather than the subtler intricacies. Millions of fans want only to believe that their hero's victory is the sole product of his virtuosity and courage. They don't want to know that his car was potentially one second per lap faster than the next guy's and that the next guy was the real hero because he was only half a second slower. They don't want to know this any more than anyone wants to know the ending of the novel they're reading. F1 is meant to be an escape from the drudgery of real life and its hard facts. Fans want to believe the fairy tale, want to live vicariously in the bubble of unreality.

This was the first time in the TV era that one driver had such a margin of superiority. It hadn't mattered when it was Juan Manuel Fangio in the 1950s or Jim Clark in the '60s. But it mattered now to those who had made themselves very rich on F1's commercial success. It mattered also to those using the sport as a billboard.

As such, the fact that Schumacher and Newey did not combine forces against the rest but instead fought each other was a godsend for those concerned with the bottom line. That way, it allowed whichever decent driver – and they were all good drivers – who plonked his backside into Newey's car to be sold as Schuey's rival. And so TV got its story.

Yet even that deeper analysis of the simplified story sold for TV consumption is itself a simplification. In truth, there was an F1 driver

Michael Schumacher takes time in a post-race collecting area to suss out some details of the Adrian Newey-designed McLaren MP4-14 as Newey talks to Mika Häkkinen, his lead driver, in the background.

of comparable ability to Schumacher, just as there was a designer worthy of comparison to Newey. But they were not yet in the right environments to make it obvious.

Ironically, while those controlling F1 worried about the scale of Schumacher's skills becoming too apparent, the sport's technology was such that the deconstruction of driver merit had become more feasible than ever before. Telemetry had first been used in the early 1980s as a tool to prevent volatile turbocharged engines from detonating themselves. But its application had become ever-more sophisticated, and into the 1990s digital data-logging could be used to analyse driver inputs. With his every throttle, brake and steering movement mapped against the topography of a circuit, and made available for the engineers and team owners to scrutinise, a driver had nowhere to hide.

This had profound psychological implications. Together with a whole host of other environmental changes – greater safety, older team owners, younger drivers, the demands of sponsors – it meant the drivers cast a less swashbuckling swathe than in previous decades. Time was when the drivers were seen as pirates who accepted no authority over their lives, their choice of a lethal profession the very embodiment of free will. Now, with their every move in the car leaving its electronic trace, there was an external tool of control over them. In the search for ever-more speed, the driver had been partly tamed – more employee than hired gun.

So while TV was constantly being sold a story of personalities, the sport itself was evolving technologies that took more of that commodity away. It was this conflict that led the FIA to ban all electronic driver aids – traction control, launch control, ABS braking, active differentials, four-wheel steering, set-ups that could be varied from corner to corner, all of which had been raced or tested – for 1994. 'Option 13' – software capable of triggering the banned launch control – was discovered on Schumacher's Benetton part-way through that year and paranoia ran riot among the other teams. Conspiracies, collusions and dark forces were everywhere. Some even wondered if Senna had been competing against an illegal car at Imola.

Concurrent with the 1994 ban on driver aids was the reintroduction of fuel stops; they had been disallowed for the previous 10 years. This opened up a new competitive dimension, making for a kaleidoscope of possibilities that played perfectly into the creative minds of Benetton's Ross Brawn and Pat Symonds, who together weaved the race strategies of Schumacher's first two world championships, 1994 and '95, in cars designed by Rory Byrne. Both times Schumacher triumphed over an ostensibly faster Newey-designed Williams driven by Damon Hill, sometimes simply because he could more than make up the difference, other times because Benetton outsmarted Williams in the new strategy game. Still other times you couldn't see the join where Schuey's genius and Brawn's

FAR LEFT: Apart from a few races in 1991, Michael Schumacher and Alain Prost faced each other only in 1993, the year of Prost's fourth world title. Eight years later Schumacher would pass Prost's record of 51 Grand Prix victories.

LEFT: Flavio Briatore brought gossip-page popularity to the sport as the man in charge of the brash Benetton team as of mid-1989. His background was a mystery. He happily confessed that his knowledge of the sport's history and technical matters was non-existent. Yet he had a shrewd feel for the running of a team.

overlapped, couldn't tell if an improbable timing of pit stops had only been made to work through the driver's ability to stretch the envelope of the possible.

The story needed a new twist and Schumacher provided it by leaving Benetton for the glorious façade of Ferrari. He was recruited by the Italian team's sporting director, Jean Todt. Unsurprisingly, the idea was first suggested to him by a certain B.C. Ecclestone Esq.

Given its facilities, resources and name upon which to trade, Ferrari had dramatically underachieved through the previous decade-and-a-half. As a brand, Ferrari was F1's ace in the hole. As a competitive force, it was limp. Schumacher magicked the odd win from his new red car in 1996, but it was hopelessly inadequate against Williams's latest Newey-penned weapon and Hill became a world champion, just like his late dad, Graham. For 1997 Todt dipped his hand into Benetton once more and recruited the missing parts of the package: Brawn and Byrne. The Benetton triangle was reunited in red, Schumacher the inspiration, Brawn the glue. And Byrne? Byrne was the man with a lower profile than Newey but comparable genius.

All the time the power brokers had worried about Senna or Schumacher combining with Newey, they apparently overlooked the fact that Schumacher was already in partnership with a design mind just as potent. Byrne's Benettons hadn't been as consistently quick as the Newey Williams' – but just as a driver needs a top car, so a

designer needs a top team. Benetton was a younger enterprise than Williams or McLaren, still building its relationships. Now that process would have to build momentum all over again at Ferrari, but with Todt at the helm taking away the traditional sting of politics in the Italian team, this was now a place of virtually unlimited potential. The balls were lining up better than they ever had in the days of Enzo Ferrari. It just needed time.

Meantime, while Newey's cars racked up the titles – Jacques Villeneuve won for Williams in 1997 – he and the Williams team were enduring the nightmare of an outside world, desperate to find someone to blame for Senna's death, applying its inappropriate logic to a sport of extremes it could never hope to understand. In the midst of it all Newey sought to have his stature confirmed by his employers, Frank Williams and Patrick Head, and was left disappointed. He defected to McLaren. Almost from the moment it happened, McLaren's star rose and Williams's fell.

Newey provided the final piece of the jigsaw for the otherwise formidable McLaren-Mercedes camp. Helped by relatively radical technical regulation changes for 1998 that wiped everyone's slates clean, he was able to provide the team's lead driver, Mika Häkkinen, with a tool that finally allowed him to express his enormous talent to the full. The Finn was the one peer Schumacher respected as an equal…

Häkkinen duly nailed the F1 titles of 1998 and '99.

FAR LEFT: Ron Dennis and Frank Williams confer. They were two of the three team principals who tried to rebel against Bernie Ecclestone's financial control of the sport in the late 1990s.

LEFT: Frenchman Jean Todt was recruited by Ferrari in 1993. As its sporting director, this former rally co-driver was a cornerstone in the team's future success. "He acts like a sponge," says a former colleague. "He absorbs all the external pressures and allows those inside the team a clear working space." Exactly what was required in the notoriously political team.

BOTTOM LEFT: Young guns Michael Schumacher and Mika Häkkinen made their F1 debuts in 1991. They had several F3 battles behind them – and some epic F1 duels ahead of them.

RIGHT: The Williams of Alain Prost and Damon Hill are leading on the opening lap of the 1993 European Grand Prix at Donington Park – but the man on the move is Ayrton Senna. Here his McLaren (8) passes Karl Wendlinger's Sauber (29), having already overtaken Michael Schumacher's Benetton into the first corner. Before the lap was out Senna had passed both Williams, too. Reckoned by many to be the greatest opening lap in F1's history, it laid the foundation of a fabulous, against-the-odds victory in extreme weather conditions.

Ayrton Senna, Alain Prost and Michael Schumacher during the 1993 South African Grand Prix at Kyalami. Prost won, Senna finished second and Schumacher retired after tangling with Senna. The three dominant drivers of the modern era have – as of the end of 2004 – 14 world championships and 175 Grand Prix victories between them.

LEFT: Michael Schumacher won 19 times with Benetton, and had a further victory removed when he was disqualified from the 1994 Belgian Grand Prix.

RIGHT: Jacques Villeneuve won the 1997 world championship after a final-round showdown with Michael Schumacher. In an attempt to keep Villeneuve behind him Schumacher committed a desperate professional foul. But it was his Ferrari that ended in the gravel trap, not Villeneuve's Williams. Here Jacques' mechanics get nto the spirit of his recent hair-colouring policy.

FOLLOWING SPREAD:
TOP LEFT: Schumacher with the architect of many of his wins, Ferrari's Manchester-born technical director Ross Brawn.

BOTTOM LEFT: Adrian Newey and Ron Dennis discuss how to stop the Ferrari steamroller.

RIGHT: Schumacher stands forlorn at Jerez in 1997, the title lost. He would also be officially stripped of the points (all 78 of them) he'd accrued that season as a punishment for his collision with title rival Villeneuve.

Jordan's Heinz-Harald Frentzen celebrates his victory at the 1999 Italian Grand Prix. He had already won that year's French Grand Prix, and so became an outside contender for the world championship. This was the last time an independent constructor, i.e. unallied to a car manufacturer, was able to form such a challenge. Thereafter, increasing manufacturer competition ensured the ante was upped.

BELOW: Ferrari fans fly the *Il Cavallino Rampante* flag at Monza.

RIGHT: Michael Schumacher's home fans are not as well-served by his victories as might be expected: he has won at Hockenheim only three times in 12 attempts.

LEFT: Jean Alesi's Ferrari 412T2 (27) triggered this incident on the opening lap of the 1995 Monaco Grand Prix by trying to go into Ste Devote, the first corner, three abreast with team-mate Gerhard Berger and the Williams FW17-Renault of David Coulthard. The race was red-flagged and restarted.

ABOVE: After winning the 1997 world championship at Jerez despite the best – and worst – efforts of Michael Schumacher, Jacques Villeneuve could afford to be magnanimous: "I guess the steering wheel must have slipped through his hands."

ABOVE: Jacques Villeneuve, son of the late Gilles, made his F1 debut in 1996 for Williams. As newly crowned American CART champion, he tested for Williams in 1995 at Silverstone. The team was initially ambivalent about his performance, but F1 boss Bernie Ecclestone – keen to have a major North American presence in his championship – reportedly convinced Frank Williams to take him on.

RIGHT: Twice in 1995 Damon Hill attempted to pass title rival Michael Schumacher, and both times he botched it, taking both men out. This is the second occasion, at Monza. Schumacher never gave the impression that he held Hill's abilities in high regard and at this moment he clearly feels the need to convey this to him.

FOLLOWING SPREAD:
Eddie Irvine experiences the dreaded refuelling fire in his Jordan-Peugeot at the Belgian Grand Prix of 1995. It was quickly extinguished and no one was hurt, but it brought home the inherent dangers of the refuelling strategy that had been reintroduced by the FIA in 1994 in an attempt to liven up the racing.

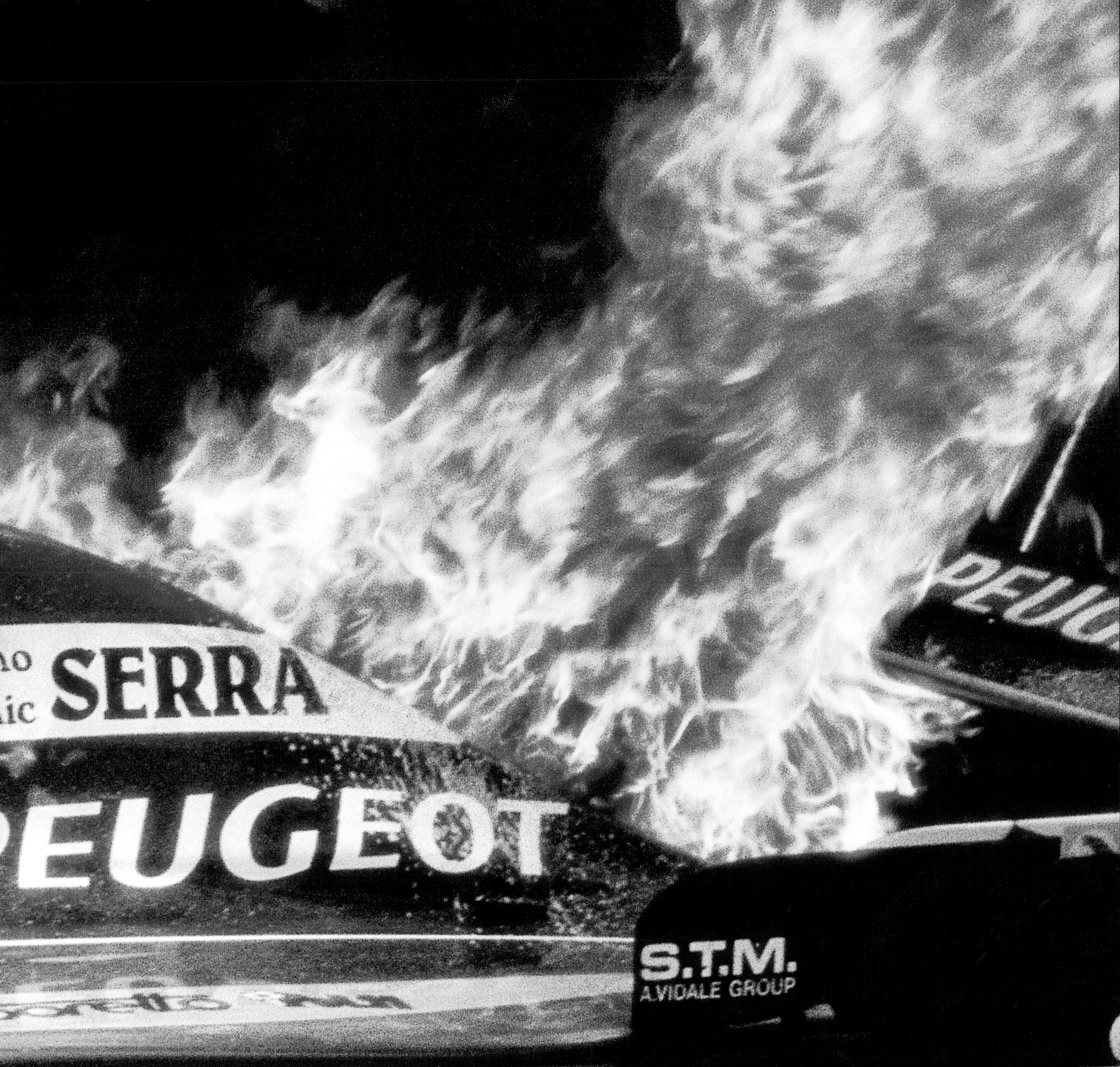

SERRA
PEUGEOT
S.T.M.
A.VIDALE GROUP

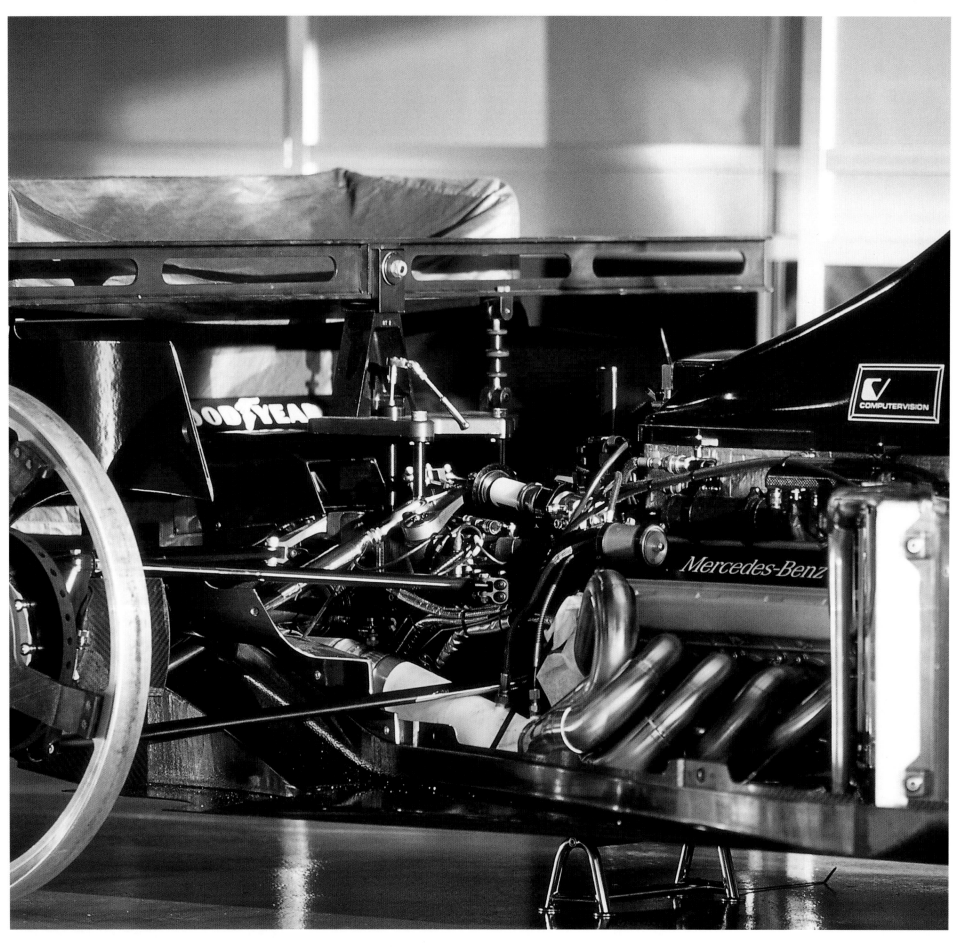

LEFT: Mercedes V10, model FO110F, in the back of the 1997 McLaren MP4-12. Designed and built by Mario Illien's Ilmor company, these units set the standard of the time for both power and lightness and were believed to be the first of the 3-litre normally aspirated engines to breach the 800bhp barrier.

TOP RIGHT: A Ferrari mechanic adjusts one of the team's V10 engines. For 29 consecutive years Ferraris were powered by 12-cylinder engines, but the 10-cylinder family, conceived and designed under the direction of Paolo Martinelli, has enjoyed unprecedented success since its introduction in 1996.

BOTTOM RIGHT: A Williams-Renault is fettled. Renault, together with Honda, pioneered the V10 format of F1 engine, first racing it in 1989. In time the layout became universally adopted.

A 1991 qualifying session gets the green light. An F1 pit lane is a busy, frantic place where you need to keep your wits about you. After a number of incidents that left mechanics injured, a speed limit, which varies depending on the circuit, was introduced in 1994. So there will be no repeat of Ayrton Senna's fastest lap in the 1993 European Grand Prix at Donington, Park, which was set on the lap he decided to abort a tyre change right at the last second.

Mika Häkkinen took his second consecutive world championship in 1999, his task made easier by the mid-season leg-breaking injury of Michael Schumacher. But there were times when Häkkinen seemed vulnerable to self-created pressure. At both the San Marino and Italian Grands Prix, he crashed his McLaren out of apparently commanding leads. He took the title by a scant two points over Ferrari's Eddie Irvine, though without these two critical errors the gap would have been 23 points, a much more accurate reflection of his speed. Häkkinen's moniker came to be 'The Ice Man' because of his coolness under pressure and a characteristic Scandinavian lack of outward emotion. It was ironic that each of his 1999 accidents came when under no great pressure on the track, almost as if he was fighting only with himself. In the aftermath of the second of them, at Monza, the emotionless façade melted too: he angrily threw down his gloves, then sat and cried. Early in 2000 he spoke a little about the emotional stress that fighting for two titles had caused him, and commented: "I don't ever want to go through that again." He narrowly lost out to Schumacher in a 2000 title showdown and retired, exhausted, at the end of 2001. A suspension breakage in Melbourne, the first race of the 2001 season, caused him a heavy accident. He was uninjured but was sent to a local hospital for a checkup. The last time he had been to an Australian hospital was in 1995 when he was fighting for his life after a tyre puncture-induced accident. By 2001 he had recently become a father for the first time. Suddenly, his thoughts became preoccupied with retirement. At the Monaco Grand Prix of that year he told team boss Ron Dennis he wanted to quit, there and then. Dennis talked him out of it. Häkkinen retired that race complaining of difficult handling, but no fault was found with his car afterwards. Yet just a few races

later, he was majestic in the British Grand Prix and dominated the event. He was similarly impressive in winning at Indianapolis, his penultimate Grand Prix.

LEFT: Michael Schumacher's Ferrari F300 at Imola in 1998. This car was not as quick as Adrian Newey's McLaren MP4-13 of that year, while Ferrari's Goodyear tyres were generally not as competitive as the Bridgestones on the McLaren. But Schumacher still carried the title fight to Mika Häkkinen. The regulations loophole that allowed ugly sidepod-mounted winglets was closed after this race.

RIGHT: Mika Häkkinen clinched the 1998 world championship with a dominant drive in the final race of the year, Japan. Eddie Irvine and David Coulthard acknowledge his new status.

FAR RIGHT: Williams's fortunes took a steep dive in 1998. From habitual title challengers, the team failed to win a race, hit by the double blow of engine supplier Renault pulling out of F1 and the defection of aerodynamicist Adrian Newey to McLaren. The following year was no better. Alex Zanardi, a dominant and compelling force in the American CART series, signed for the team, and endured a fraught year, scoring just one point. His FW21 is craned away after crashing out of the Canadian race.

TOP LEFT: Ferrari's Michael Schumacher and Jean Todt, two keystones to the greatest period of sustained success for any team in the sport's history. Schumacher needs a comfortable family atmosphere within his team to give his best; Todt specialises in providing exactly that.

BOTTOM LEFT: Eddie Irvine came within an ace of winning the 1999 world championship, stepping up as Ferrari team leader after Schumacher's Silverstone accident. Ultimately, he was beaten by McLaren's Mika Häkkinen.

RIGHT: Schumacher's Ferrari F300 cuts a swathe through a wet Monza during practice for the 1998 Italian Grand Prix. He went on to win the race from team-mate Irvine, thereby giving the squad its first 1-2 on home soil for a decade, illustrating that the process of transforming Ferrari from faded has-beens to world-beaters was proceeding nicely. Although this victory brought Schumacher into title contention, it was very much against the run of play and the McLaren of that year was generally the faster car. Every season from 1996 through to 2002, however, each Ferrari was more competitive than its predecessor and, by 2000, the run of Schumacher's driver titles was under way.

FOLLOWING SPREAD:
LEFT: Damon Hill had been unable to parlay the speed of his Adrian Newey-designed Williams into championship success against Schumacher in 1994 or '95. But in 1996, with Schumacher joining an underdeveloped Ferrari, Hill had his big chance. And he seized it, winning the title from his only serious rival, rookie team-mate Jacques Villeneuve. However, even that was not enough in the opinion of Frank Williams and Patrick Head: Hill was replaced for 1997.

RIGHT: Ralf Schumacher's Jordan hits the Montreal barriers – hard. In his rookie F1 season of 1997, Michael's younger brother wasn't always fully in control of his undeniable speed. His elder sibling's brilliance set him an impossible standard to be measured against.

1990 – HIGH-NOSE AERODYNAMICS

The Tyrrell 019, with aerodynamics by Jean-Claude Migeot, pioneered the high-nose design (top left). This encourages airflow to travel beneath the car and so make the rear diffuser far more effective. This brought a big increase in downforce for no penalty in drag.

1992 – ACTIVE RIDE & ELECTRONIC GIZMOS

Active ride did away with conventional springs and replaced them with computer-controlled, electro-hydraulic actuators that kept the car completely level at all times, eliminating roll and pitch. The potential aerodynamic advantages this brought were enormous as the car could be kept at its peak attitude (downforce increases exponentially as the car's underside gets closer to the ground). Lotus tried a system as early as 1983 but the analogue control systems of the time were not up to the task. In 1987 both Lotus and Williams won races with active-suspension cars, but although the control systems were now digital there was still not sufficient processing power to bring a significant advantage over conventional suspension. The breakthrough was made with the much more powerful processing of the Williams FW14B of 1992 (top right). Finally, the potential of the technology became apparent as this car was often up to two seconds per lap faster than its opposition.

1994 – GIZMOS BANNED. RETURN OF FUEL STOPS & THE STRATEGY GAME

The governing body banned active ride and the full range of electronic gizmos: traction control, ABS braking, fully automated pre-programmed gearshifts, variable chassis settings from corner to corner. At the same time it allowed teams to again make fuel stops during a race. This brought a new competitive element into play as teams tried to outwit each other with fuel strategies, the number of stops and their timings. Pit crew performance became critical.

1994 – SAFETY CHANGES

In the wake of Ayrton Senna's fatal accident in the San Marino Grand Prix, several changes were made: a wooden plank on the underside of the car restricted how close to the ground the cars could run, thereby impeding their aerodynamic efficiency; cockpit sides had to be built up and incorporate a padded head-protecting area (bottom left); pit lane speed limits were introduced.

1995 – NEW FORMULA

MAXIMUM ENGINE CAPACITY: 3 litres normally aspirated

1998 – GROOVED TYRES & NARROW TRACK

As part of the ongoing legislation to control speeds, slick tyres were outlawed via a rule requiring grooved tyres (bottom right) to limit mechanical grip. At the same time, and with the same aim, the maximum track (the width between a car's wheel centres) was reduced. Lap times initially increased by around 2.5 seconds.

2001 – LIMITED RETURN OF GIZMOS

The governing body despaired of being able to police the software of the teams and so allowed the return of traction and launch control as well as electronically controlled differentials that aided the direction-changing process.

2003 – QUALIFYING WITH RACE FUEL

Single-car qualifying was introduced, giving drivers just one lap in which to set their grid time. In addition, fuel could not be added between qualifying and race, forcing drivers to qualify with enough fuel on board to do their first race stint. This brought a new element to the strategy game.

2004 – LAUNCH CONTROL REBANNED

The governing body decided it could, after all, police launch control. So it was rebanned, requiring the drivers to once again control their own starts.

Record-breakers or Ballbreakers?

A confluence of circumstances posed F1 some heady challenges as it headed flat-out into the 21st century. On a macro scale, it was in danger of becoming a victim of its own commercial success, with serious unrest arising from several points of internal conflict. Yet like a virus unconcerned with the health of its host, on a micro level the participants couldn't but help maximise their own competitive advantage, as any good racing addict should. What this opened up in an era when car manufacturers had upped the financial ante was a huge division between the haves and have-nots that threatened to recreate levels of conflict last seen in the early 1980s. It's also made for the most sustained period of one-sided competition the sport has ever seen as Ferrari – the team with the most of everything – just did what comes naturally.

Whatever shock F1 had received from Ayrton Senna's death, what it had not bargained on was the sport's enhanced growth in the wake of the tragedy. Already-enormous TV figures shot up, and such was the sport's marketing reach that those car manufacturers not yet involved questioned whether they could afford to stay out any longer.

By the mid-1990s the tobacco industry that had largely fuelled F1 in the 1970s and '80s was no longer the sport's biggest benefactor – the car manufacturers were. As ever, F1 simply draws on whatever the environment offers up. The irony was that it became more addicted to the manufacturers than it had ever been to tobacco. Manufacturers, as well as providing the engines for the array of independent teams, also supplied the cash that drove the technology race at a breakneck pace, quadrupling and more the size of the teams. Manufacturers also began buying equity in teams or, in the case of Toyota and Renault, became teams in their own right.

Indeed, the manufacturer money flooded in perhaps faster than Max Mosley and Bernie Ecclestone – the twin towers of F1 – would have liked. Where was their iron-fisted control and manoeuvrability if the manufacturers acquired power, as they inevitably would, even if they didn't at first use it?

And there was further trouble brewing as Bernie tried to lay the ground for extricating himself and releasing the fruits of his labours and brilliance as mortality loomed. In the late 1990s the books went public for an attempted flotation of the sport and certain key team owners were outraged when they saw what lay within them. Bernie had made these men rich, and while they still possessed the racer's addiction that brought them in, they were now on more than nodding terms with business. So when they

For Ferrari fans, the first four years of the 21st century have outstripped anything they've ever experienced before. The last time the team was as dominant was for a much shorter period, 1952–53.

discovered how much richer they and their teams could be, they were upset. This disquiet rumbles on today.

The flotation sank without trace and instead a share of the business was sold – to a TV company. That also upset the manufacturers. They didn't like the idea that their wonderful marketing platform could be owned and controlled by a body unrelated to the car industry. They were even more upset when this share of the business ended up in the hands of three commercial banks after the buyer went bust. Then the banks got upset when they realised how little control they had over a business they owned a significant chunk of.

The cause of all this trouble was, oddly, that F1 was too successful, had grown too big too quickly. The sport was ever-more unwieldy. Ecclestone's management of it had been brilliant for decades, but now he found himself at the controls of a Jumbo, not a Cessna. In the meantime, a vital tool of control was snatched away from those running the sport: tobacco revenue, a hefty bulwark against the march of the manufacturers, was about to be stubbed out. The advertising of its wares was banned by European law as from 2006.

F1 began to spread its geographical tentacles, not only to get around the tobacco ban but also because tiger economy governments saw it as a legitimisation of their commercial cred: Malaysia, Bahrain and China hosted their first Grands Prix in opulent surroundings; India began to make interested noises.

On-track, Ferrari won the constructors' world championship in 1999, its first title of any sort for 16 years. But that was just the lapping of the water over a previously unburstable dam of British teamwork, skill and ingenuity. It was about to break completely, unable any more to contain the onslaught of talent, drive and money of the reconstituted Italian team.

Although Michael Schumacher's genius had disguised the fact, it had taken a few years for Ross Brawn and Rory Byrne to make Ferrari the team it should always have been. They had arrived to find a technical desert behind the beautiful façade – albeit with some glittering jewels. One was the name, perhaps the most charismatic brand in the marketing world; generating the income for whatever was needed was not going to be a problem. Another was the fantastic potential integration of a team that made its own engines.

Ever since Cooper had revolutionised the sport in the late 1950s, its *garagiste* approach of subcontracting and assembling

FAR LEFT: **There's always been a party atmosphere at Interlagos, a reason for hope. Nowadays the Brazilians shout for their hometown hero, Ferrari's Rubens Barrichello. But he has yet to bring them the victory they crave…**

LEFT: **… he has won elsewhere, of course. 'Rubinho' celebrates a rare victory over Michael Schumacher in the 2002 European Grand Prix at the Nürburgring. Despite being the clear number two in Ferrari's pecking order, the likeable Brazilian has pushed Schumacher harder than any of his previous team-mates, ever more so as the Ferraris have improved over the years and become 'easier' to drive.**

had held sway. But it was only allowed to by Ferrari's squandering of its in-built advantage of integration. The dovetailing of a newly technology-led Ferrari with a sport that had become vastly more complex, where ever-smaller margins of advantage were being chased – and where, therefore, integration between engine and chassis was a key area – finally released that structural advantage.

Mix in the talents of Schumacher, Byrne, Brawn and Jean Todt and the tide finally turned in 2000. When Schumacher defeated McLaren's Mika Häkkinen in Japan to take that year's world championship, it marked the passing of the era of the specialist constructor. The fractured British team structure – even among manufacturer-backed teams like McLaren – that had flourished ever since the time of Cooper was now a liability. Ferrari was soon winning like no team had ever won before, dominating for year upon year.

Among its rivals the tension rose; it was tough to call whether Williams's partnership with engine supplier BMW was more fraught than that of McLaren's with Mercedes. Oh, there were moments, days when the McLaren momentum still carried Häkkinen along, but he retired, exhausted, at the end of 2001. Then there was the

combination of BMW horsepower and the wildcat racer Juan Pablo Montoya, the most combative since Nigel Mansell and arguably the best overtaker the sport has ever seen. But there's been nothing to prevent the Reds prevailing – even to the extent of Austria 2002, where Ferrari triggered an outcry by turning a dull demonstration of its superiority into a travesty by instructing race-leading Rubens Barrichello to pull over for Schumacher within yards of the finish line. Here was a classic example of how racers don't even understand the macro, let alone consider it. That's how intense the micro is: more, always more.

If at the end of its 1980s crisis the sport was revealed as immature but with commercial potential, this time it was as a vastly successful and in some ways very slick commercial entity – but one which was struggling to cope with a rapid transformation of its structure, from entrepreneurial to managerial.

And so it becomes more and more out of kilter, this huge commercial entity. But in the middle of it all they race on, just as they would if every last sponsor pulled out, every last manufacturer was gone. The commercial world is merely the sport's steering wheel. It kids itself if it thinks it's the engine. That is provided by addiction. And that is F1's true magnificence.

TOP LEFT: **Modern F1 teams the size of armies generate files and files of information. Collating it and sifting through it can throw up that small but crucial advantage every team craves. Nothing is thrown away or dismissed as unimportant.**

BOTTOM LEFT: **Michael Schumacher's overalls – used for one race, maybe a test, then either auctioned or given away.**

TOP RIGHT: **McLaren-Mercedes engine covers glint in the gathering dusk at Budapest in 2000, ready for battle with Ferrari the next day.**

BOTTOM RIGHT: **Ever-more intricate design chasing ever-smaller margins. A 'chimney' on the Ferrari F2002 deflects hot air from the radiators away from the airflow to the rear wing – and incorporated within it is the engine's exhaust outlet.**

PREVIOUS SPREAD:

TOP LEFT: **Rubens Barrichello is being treated as the winner of the 2002 Austrian Grand Prix even though – acting under team orders – he surrendered his lead within yards of the finish line to Schumacher. The incident caused a furore that pinpointed the sport's concerns about Ferrari's dominance.**

BOTTOM LEFT: **Michael Schumacher and 'his team'. Flanking him are wife Corinna – former girlfriend of Heinz-Harald Frentzen – and manager Willi Weber. Behind him are Ferrari's sporting director, test driver and number two driver: Jean Todt, Luca Badoer and Barrichello.**

RIGHT: **Barrichello takes centre stage – for real this time – after his dominant victory in the 2002 Hungarian Grand Prix at Budapest.**

TOP LEFT: **Ross Brawn**, Ferrari's technical director, served his racing apprenticeship at Williams. He moved to the Beatrice F1 team in 1985, and when that folded joined Arrows as its chief designer. He followed that with a spell designing Tom Walkinshaw's Jaguar sports-racers, which is where he first met Schumacher, who was driving for the rival Mercedes team. "I could see then that Michael was a bit special," says Brawn. "Our Jaguar was much faster, but every time Michael got in the Mercedes he was able to give us something to worry about. Then, when their other guys got in, it faded again." Brawn's partnership with Walkinshaw led to a return to F1 when the latter bought a stake in the Benetton team. Its incumbent designer was Rory Byrne, with whom Brawn soon forged a close working relationship. Benetton then recruited Schumacher in 1991. This trio have since won seven world drivers' titles, two with Benetton and five with Ferrari.

BOTTOM LEFT: Ferrari designer Byrne is congratulated by company president Luca di Montezemolo.

RIGHT: It may look totally chaotic but every single element of a team's performance is choreographed to perfection. Those who grew up with Ferrari pit stops that resembled scenes from a Marx Brothers film would not recognise this as the same team.

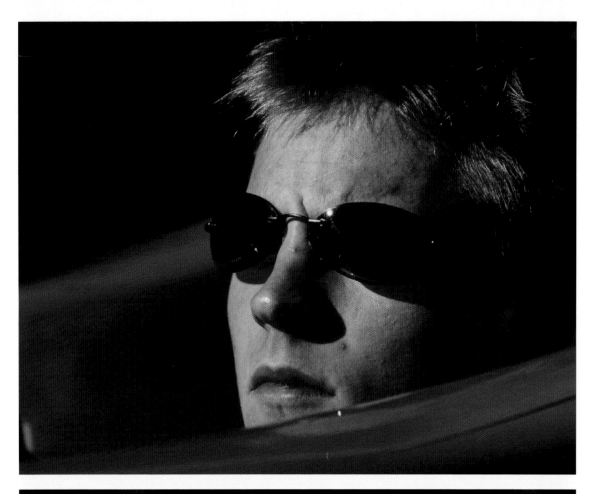

TOP LEFT: **Kimi Raikkonen, along with Fernando Alonso, represents the cutting edge of the generation of drivers set to take over from Michael Schumacher. His startling turn of speed is blended with an icy coolness under pressure.**

BOTTOM LEFT: **Takuma Sato emerged from his rookie F1 season, 2002, as the man likely to finally give Japan a Grand Prix-winning driver.**

BOTTOM LEFT: Mika Häkkinen, world champion in 1998 and '99, was a complex character and a stunningly fast driver. He retired from F1 at the end of the 2001, tired of the personal stress that the sport was causing him.

RIGHT: **As Juan Pablo Montoya waits his turn in one-lap qualifying, he watches his monitor and sees Cristiano da Matta, the Brazilian former Indycar champion, spin his Toyota.**

FAR RIGHT: **Michael Schumacher takes victory in the 2002 British Grand Prix, scene of the very first world championship Grand Prix in 1950 – and of Ferrari's first championship-status victory the following year.**

FOLLOWING SPREAD:
With a higher concentration of millionaires than any other place in the world, Monte Carlo is a natural habitat for F1. This is the 2003 race. The Swimming Pool Complex that juts into the harbour was first 'navigated' by F1 cars in 1973.

LEFT: The Williams FW24-BMWs of Juan Pablo Montoya and Ralf Schumacher out-accelerate Michael Schumacher's Ferrari F2002 away from the grid at the start of the 2002 Italian Grand Prix. The previous day Montoya had recorded the fastest-ever F1 qualifying lap, averaging 161.449mph around Monza, his engine revving to over 19,000rpm, a first for F1.

TOP RIGHT: A tyre technician uses a probe to measure track temperature, a critical element in squeezing performance from the car.

BOTTOM RIGHT: Nick Heidfeld's Sauber drives over the yard-wide strip of bricks on the Indianapolis start/finish straight in 2002. The entire 2.5 miles of this 'oval' circuit was paved with bricks in 1909 after the original crushed-stone-and-asphalt surface broke up badly. This strip was left in recognition of the track's legacy when it finally received an asphalt surface. The venue of the famous Indy 500 was first used by F1 in 2000 as part of the category's most determined bid yet to crack the tough American market.

FOLLOWING SPREAD:
LEFT: Schumacher's crash helmet colour scheme has evolved over the seasons, becoming progressively more red as it became clearer that he would never leave Ferrari – and to differentiate it from Rubens Barrichello's.

RIGHT: Even in the wet a modern F1 tyre generates plenty of heat.

LEFT: Fernando Alonso became the youngest F1 winner when he triumphed in the 2003 Hungarian Grand Prix for Renault. He was 22 years and 26 days old, beating the record held by the late Bruce McLaren for the previous 45 years. Alonso's biggest strength is an amazing facility to lap flat-out from start to finish, a relentless quality reminiscent of Schumacher.

ABOVE: Fighting deteriorating tyre grip, Juan Pablo Montoya spins his Williams FW24-BMW during the 2002 European Grand Prix while trying to fend off David Coulthard's McLaren MP4-17-Mercedes for fourth place.

TOP LEFT: Bahrain's first Grand Prix in 2004 represented a great opportunity for the country to advertise its credentials for investment. An increasing number of races away from the traditional F1 base of continental Europe were being subsidised by governments. Fernando Alonso races across the exotic desert background in his Renault.

BOTTOM LEFT: China's new Shanghai circuit – constructed specially for F1 – set astounding new standards of opulence as the sport visited the country for the first time in 2004. Ironically, it came at a time when the sport itself was facing an economic crisis.

RIGHT: It's hard to argue with the message on Michael Schumacher's pit board as he completes the 2004 Belgian Grand Prix. He was beaten on the day by McLaren's Kimi Raikkonen, but still secured his seventh title.

FOLLOWING SPREAD: Michael Schumacher broke Alain Prost's all-time record of 51 wins when he won the 2001 Belgian Grand Prix. Prost meanwhile was enduring a second career less glittering than his first – as owner of a struggling F1 team. In this race Prost driver Luciano Burti suffered a massive accident that left him concussed. With the team already £10 million in debt, Prost did not survive into the following season. Ferrari's dominance was playing its part in making survival at the wrong end of the grid a financially perilous game.